ALVERNO
INSTRUCTIONAL SERVICES CENTER

Handbook on
Supported Education

Handbook on Supported Education

Providing Services for Students with Psychiatric Disabilities

by

Karen V. Unger, M.S.W., Ed.D.
Rehabilitation Through Education
Portland, Oregon

·P A U L·H·
BROOKES
PUBLISHING C9

Baltimore • London • Toronto • Sydney

Paul H. Brookes Publishing Co.
Post Office Box 10624
Baltimore, Maryland 21285-0624

www.pbrookes.com

Copyright © 1998 by Paul H. Brookes Publishing Co., Inc.
All rights reserved.

Typeset by Barton Matheson Willse & Worthington,
Baltimore, Maryland.
Manufactured in the United States of America by
Versa Press, East Peoria, Illinois.

The suggestions in this book are not intended as a substitute for professional medical consultation. The author and publisher disclaim any liability arising directly from the use of this book.

The case studies described in this book represent actual people and circumstances. Most names have been changed to protect identities. In those cases in which the identities have not been disguised, written consent has been given.

Library of Congress Cataloging-in-Publication Data

Unger, Karen V.
    Handbook on supported education : providing services for students with psychiatric disabilities / Karen V. Unger.
        p.   cm.
    Includes bibliographical references (p.) and index.
    ISBN 1-55766-352-1
    1. Mentally ill—Education (Higher)—United States—Handbooks, manuals, etc. 2. Mentally ill—Services for—United States—Handbooks, manuals, etc.
LC4826.U54   1998
371.94—DC21   98-10493
                                                                          CIP

British Library Cataloguing in Publication data are available from the British Library.

Contents

About the Author

Karen V. Unger, M.S.W., Ed.D., President, Rehabilitation Through Education, Post Office Box 82176, Portland, Oregon 97282-0176

Karen V. Unger has worked in the fields of mental health and education as a teacher, a trainer, an administrator, and a researcher. During her tenure at Boston University's Center for Psychiatric Rehabilitation (1981–1993), she developed and defined the concept of *supported education*. While at the center, she completed two research and demonstration projects testing the efficacy of supported education and then disseminated the concept across the United States.

Dr. Unger is currently completing a field-initiated research project funded by the National Institute on Disability Rehabilitation and Research through the University of Arizona. The project is designed to examine the long-term outcomes of supported education. She is also working with various education programs to apply the concept of supported education to the transition process for youth with serious emotional and behavior disorders.

Dr. Unger earned her doctorate in education from Boston University, her master's of social work from Arizona State University, her master's degree in psychology from Chapman College, and her master's degree in education from California State Polytechnic University. Her undergraduate work was completed at North Dakota State University in English. She has published numerous journal articles and book chapters and has spoken at conferences throughout the United States and abroad.

Foreword

Handbook on Supported Education: Providing Services for Students with Psychiatric Disabilities may be the most important new resource in several years for personnel working with students with disabilities in higher education. While the number of students with all disabilities has grown substantially over the years, the number of students with identified mental illnesses seems to have grown exponentially. This book represents the single best source of information currently available regarding the issues, needs, and support of this group of individuals.

For some time, bewildered college administrators and disability services personnel have been asking, "Where did all of these students with psychiatric disabilities come from? What are we supposed to do with them (for them)?" This text provides very specific information and guidance in response to these genuine pleas for help. Chapter 1 provides a historical perspective on the inclusion of students with psychiatric disabilities in the postsecondary environment. Chapter 2 gives a thorough explanation of the nature of mental disorders in nonmedical terms and in a nonmedical perspective. Chapter 3 provides information on treatment and interventions commonly employed with individuals who manifest a wide range of psychiatric disabilities. For postsecondary personnel who have traditionally shied away from asking too many questions regarding a diagnosis of mental illness because they were afraid they would not understand—and did not want to hear!—the answers, these chapters provide invaluable assistance in reading reports from mental health professionals and understanding the impact of a student's mental illness on the educational experience.

Chapter 4 offers an excellent review of legal obligations and applicable case law regarding students with disabilities in higher education. Dr. Unger has done an impressive job of detailing the information specific to students with psychiatric disabilities; perhaps more important, she has included in this review pertinent case law regarding students with other disabilities and suggested the implications of these cases for the issues surrounding individuals with psychiatric disabilities. Chapter 5 addresses the role and responsibility of the postsecondary institution in providing accommodations and services, touching on issues ranging from eligibility/admissions and confidentiality to the necessary skills, operating values, and practices of the service provider. Chapter 6 provides a straightforward review of the health and safety concerns most commonly cited as the reason for limiting the participation of individuals with mental illness in higher education. The very specific recommendations for classroom management strategies and the guidelines suggested for policy development make this a "must read" for faculty and administrators who are interacting with real students and, thus, need real answers.

Chapter 7 offers practical advice for mental health personnel who work with postsecondary students and potential students with psychiatric disabilities. The "Guidelines for Assisting Students Who Attend College," and the review of model programs for supported education provide practical tools that can be employed in designing and implementing such services. Chapters 8, 9, and 10 offer important information and support to consumers while providing valuable insight to service providers and other postsecondary personnel working with such students.

Colleges and universities have long understood that they are legally responsible for providing equal access to education for students with disabilities. However, when the disability involved is some form of mental illness, administrators, faculty, and service providers are often uncertain as to when and how that mandate for equal access should be applied.

Handbook on Supported Education: Providing Services for Students with Psychiatric Disabilities takes our understanding of the questions— and the answers!—to a new level. Dr. Unger makes a persuasive case for the feasibility and appropriateness of supported education for students with psychiatric disabilities. Now it is our job to make it happen!

Jane Jarrow, Ph.D.
President
Disability Access Information and Support (DAIS)
Columbus, Ohio

Preface

All of us who provide or use supported education services are part of a quiet revolution—a revolution that is changing the way in which people with mental illness are perceived, either by themselves or by others. As more and more people with mental illness return to post-secondary education, previously held stigmas and perceptions are being broken down. People with mental illness want to learn new knowledge and gain new understanding that will enhance their quality of life, and learning new skills will enable these individuals to develop careers as well as hold meaningful jobs.

This quiet revolution is slow, but it is strong. It began with the dissatisfaction of people with mental illness who wanted a better life. It gained momentum when their dissatisfaction was officially documented by research. The revolution continued as new programs that provided the groundwork for and documented the fact that returning to college was a viable option for people with mental illness emerged. The passage of the Americans with Disabilities Act (ADA) of 1990 (PL 101-336) was a timely boost to Section 504 of the Rehabilitation Act of 1973 (PL 93-112), which stated that institutions who received federal funds could not discriminate against individuals with disabilities. These laws made it even more clear that services and accommodations on college and university campuses should be made available to individuals with mental illness just as they are made available to individuals with physical or other invisible disabilities, such as acquired brain injury or learning disabilities.

New medications are also advancing the revolution. People with mental illness are no longer simply medicated in order to "quiet" their symptoms. New, improved medications target specific areas of the brain to alleviate particular symptoms, and, as a result, more and more people with mental illness are able to resume their normal functioning. Soon mental illness as we know it may no longer exist.

Returning to school is a process that helps restore people. It promotes the development of self-esteem and a new positive self-image. Education can counteract the feelings of worthlessness that many people with mental illness have internalized because of the stigmas attached to their disabilities. Education helps to develop new skills and new ways of behaving. It provides individuals with the motivation to manage symptoms and helps individuals resume a healthy lifestyle. Returning to school supports recovery.

PURPOSE

The purpose of this book is to give the reader a "how to" book. It provides ideas and methods for providing supported education services to people with mental illness and gives people who have been diagnosed with a mental illness guidelines for improving their success on college and university campuses. For those readers who are unfamiliar with symptoms of and treatments for mental illness, this book provides elementary information to demystify the myths associated with psychiatric disabilities and offers intervention alternatives to treat them. This book provides a summary of pertinent case law to document the disputes that have been raised regarding the implementation of disability law. Finally, this book is written to advocate for supported education services and to help the reader understand the meaningfulness of returning to school for the students with mental illness who have resumed their educations. Welcome to the revolution!

VOCABULARY

Vocabulary in relation to mental disorders is controversial. The disorder itself has many names, including *mental illness, mental disorder, psychiatric disability, psychological disorder, psychosocial disability, brain disorder*, and *neurobiological disorder*. The name used to refer to this disorder depends on the group one belongs to and/or how one perceives the disorder. For this book, I have elected to use *mental illness, mental disorder*, and *psychiatric disabilities* to describe the group of disorders that are described in the *Diagnostic and Statistical Manual of Mental Disorders, Fourth Edition* (American Psychiatric Association, 1994). (These are the terms I most often hear used in the field.)

The language used when referring to people with a mental illness is also controversial. No one name seems to satisfy everyone. For this book, I have tried to use the name that makes the most sense in the context in which I am writing. I have used the terms *student, consumer, client*, and *patient*. My intent is to speak most directly to as many different audiences as possible.

When I write about postsecondary education, I am referring to all institutions that provide educational, vocational, and professional training for individuals with mental illness who have completed the institutions' requirements for a secondary certificate or diploma. This includes colleges, universities, and trade and professional schools. Rather than list the type of school each time I make a reference to post-secondary education institutions, I most often use the word *college*.

REFERENCES

American Psychiatric Association. (1994). *Diagnostic and statistical manual of mental disorders* (4th ed.). Washington, DC: Author.

Americans with Disabilities Act (ADA) of 1990, PL 101-336, 42 U.S.C. §§ 12101 *et seq.*

Rehabilitation Act of 1973, PL 93-112, 29 U.S.C. §§ 701 *et seq.*

Acknowledgments

I would like to acknowledge the following individuals for reading chapters and providing feedback and advice: Linda Cooper, Steve Dougherty, Elsa Eckblaw, Deanne Gilmur, Molly Holsapple, Susan Langi, Jay Mahler, Phyllis Paulson, Debra Rades, and Tim Stringari. A special thanks to my editors, Jennifer Lazaro Kinard and Seth G. Morrison.

To the students

Handbook on
Supported Education

The Emergence of
Supported Education

A Rehabilitative Approach

My day treatment program was this house on Second Street. You didn't do anything. You could read or drink coffee, and then they'd have lunch. You could help them cook—that—and some little craft things. It was a nine-month program, but I only stayed two weeks. And as far as the vocational thing, they wanted to put you automatically in real low level jobs. (Tim, cited in Unger, 1987, p. 115)

It's amazing how much more responsible I am when the freedom is here than in a hospital setting where I'm trying to figure out how to sneak out for a joint. Because there's that control and that control makes me resentful and rebellious. Whereas at school, where I'm responsible and respected, I behave in a responsible manner. (Michael, cited in Unger, 1987, pp. 115–116)

What I like best about the university, in the sense that there's a library, a cafeteria, students—I feel at home. I feel like I belong here. I don't feel alienated; I don't feel ostracized; I don't feel stupid. If I went to a hospital or even a day program, by the mere fact that I was there means that there is something wrong with me. (Gabe, cited in Unger, 1987, p. 119)

[handwritten note: Supported Education grew out of young adults w/ MI's dissatisfaction w/ current treatment models in 80s]

_OPMENT
UCATION

_ults with mental illness became a major
___ ctitioners. These young adults with mental illness, many ___ ___ ere recently diagnosed, did not "fit" into the traditional mental health service delivery system. These individuals did not want to be grouped with older consumers who had spent much of their lives in and out of psychiatric hospitals, and they found the existing mental health services inappropriate and stigmatizing. To address the needs of these young adults with mental illness, new services ___ ___ ___ e was *supported education*.

Su___ ___ ___ ble as a result of the increasing knowle___ ___ ses. This increase was brought about b___ ___ understanding of the potential of peop___ ___ ntal illnesses. The goal of supported ___ who have a history of mental illness t___ ___ lary education. Supported education ___ successful participation in the college ___ ___ ___ tcome is for individuals with mental i___ to obtain or to return to meaningful work that is commensurate with their abilities.

[handwritten note: Goal: return to meaningful work commensurate w/ ability.]

A diagnosis of a mental illness is no longer akin to a terminal disease. Although mental illness is a very serious illness, there remains the very real possibility that with the use of appropriate medication (when necessary) and through rehabilitative and therapeutic services, people with mental illness can resume their rightful roles as workers, students, family members, and community participants. This chapter traces the changes that have occurred in the delivery of mental health services and the developments that have opened the doorways to an idea such as supported education. It also describes how supported education emerged and developed into a beneficial and successful adjunct to existing services.

The Deinstitutionalization Movement

Since the mid-1960s, there has been a dramatic shift in the way that mental illness is viewed and treated. Prior to this time, mental illness was traditionally seen as a severe disease of prolonged duration that resulted in moderate to severe disabilities (Goldman, Gattozzi, & Yawke, 1981). The term *chronically mentally ill* was used to describe individuals who had received a diagnosis of a major mental illness (National Institute of Mental Health [NIMH], 1980).

Treatment was based on the medical model that attempted to "cure" the disease through the determination of possible causes, symptom reduction and therapeutic insights, the utilization of drugs, and psychotherapy. The purpose of psychotherapy was to provide a corrective experience. Desired outcomes of the psychotherapies, in which prolonged hospitalization for intervention was often necessary, were

- Increased insight
- Resolution of disabling conflicts
- Increased self-acceptance
- More efficient techniques for cc ... problems
- General strengthening of the e ... of adequacy and security

During the late 1960s and ea ... de-veloped that more effectively cc ... il ill-nesses. People who previously h ... often were able to manage the activiti ... hospi-tals, and there was a movement ... these individuals into the community. This move... as *de-institutionalization*. By 1977, NIMH reported a 66% decrease in the number of individuals residing in state mental hospitals.

People who had resided in hospitals for years, however, needed living and treatment programs in the community. Unfortunately, communities not only did not have funds to meet this need but also were not prepared to provide the services needed by these individuals. Although community mental health centers had been established in many cities within the United States in the 1960s and 1970s, the individuals with chronic mental illness were not among their priorities. As a result, there were few resources available to the individuals being released from the hospital.

In response to this lack of services, NIMH began funding community support programs in 1980 that established some programs in local communities (NIMH, 1980). In addition, many day treatment and partial hospitalization programs, which are often found on hospital grounds, were made available to promote individuals' stabilization after brief hospital stays. As time went on and new cases of mental illnesses developed and were diagnosed in young adults, however, it became clear that these community services were not appropriate for every individual.

Defining the "Young Adult Chronic"

In the early 1980s, a group of individuals in the mental health system were identified as *young adult chronics*. These individuals had two defining characteristics: 1) They were between the ages of 18 and 35, and 2) they were described as "difficult to treat" (Bachrach, 1982a, 1982b; Pepper & Ryglewicz, 1984). The deinstitutionalization movement not only moved these people into the community but also limited the amount of time they were allowed to stay in psychiatric hospitals (NIMH, 1977). As a result, these younger adults did not adopt the learned behaviors of passivity and hopelessness that many older adults who had spent extended periods of time in hospitals did.

The young adults exhibited many of the less-positive behaviors of some of their peers, such as drinking and using drugs. They frequently chose not to use the existing day treatment programs available in the community because they did not want to be identified with the older adults who also attended these programs or because they found that the programs were not helpful to them. When they did require treatment, they often used hospital emergency rooms. Consequently, these young adults were defined as using the mental health system "inappropriately."

Many writers during the late 1970s and early 1980s expressed frustration with trying to provide services to the young adults with mental illnesses (De Forge, cited in Bachrach, 1982a; Harris & Bergman, cited in Bachrach, 1982a; Pepper, 1984). De Forge described these young adults as individuals who "confound all your treatment efforts, who will take your emergency workers and your other treatment people and run them in circles for many hours and many days, so that staff reaction to them is basically a lot of anger and frustration" (cited in Bachrach, 1982a, p. 101). In her article, Bachrach quoted Harris and Bergman: "After several rounds of bouncing between hospitals and community, no one expects these patients to change. They are treated perfunctorily . . . by a staff that is too discouraged to go through the motions" (1982a, p. 101). Pepper documented another example of the frustration felt by many service providers when interacting with young adults:

> Some of these clients had made themselves *personae non gratae* even to mental health agencies by their disruptive and incorrigible behavior. Some presented problems of recurrent serious violence in their parent's home or in the locked ward of psychiatric hospitals. Many defied diagnosis by presenting a psychiatric disorder complicated by drug abuse—or was it toxic psychosis mimicking schizophrenia? Finally, many either overtly rejected treatment or simply wandered away from the most carefully planned path of aftercare. (1984, p. 6)

These situations reflect the feelings of many service providers. Their comments also speak indirectly to the paucity of programs available for individuals between 18 and 35 years of age. The lack of suitable programs during the late 1970s and early 1980s was formally *[handwritten note: Dissatisfaction w/ services led to [...] inapp behavior?]*

documented in a study condu[...] for the Mentally Ill (NAMI) (Unger [...] tion of parents of people with mental il[...] dy indicated that 75% of the young [...] with vocational rehabilitation service [...] ial rehabilitation services, 76% were dissausried with educational services, and 63% were dissatisfied with day intervention.

The lack of suitable programs was further compounded by the increased numbers of young adults who were entering the mental health system. These individuals represented one of the fastest growing segments of individuals with mental illness in the United States. Approximately half of the individuals who received services in mental health centers were between the ages of 18 and 35 (Bassuk, 1980; Egri & Caton, 1981; Pandiani & Butterfield, 1980; Wagner, 1981). With deinstitutionalization, these young adults were returned to the community for treatment after only brief hospitalizations instead of residing in state hospitals for most of their lives. Once back in the community, one third to one half of the young adults did not show up for their initial appointments with their new community services providers. Of those who did show up, 40%–50% did not return for support after their initial sessions. Their reported rehospitalization rates were as high as 75% (Anthony, Buell, Sharratt, & Althoff, 1972).

There also were numerous studies in the early 1980s that documented the fact that young adults with mental illness did not have the skills necessary to function effectively in the community (Bachrach, 1982b; Goldman et al., 1981; Wallace et al., 1980). Young adults in the community were described by Goldman et al. (1981) as socially isolated, hostile, and alienated from family and friends. These individuals exhibited acute vulnerability to stress, repeated failures in judgment, acting-out behavior, and poor social and psychological functioning. Bachrach (1982b) and Wallace et al. (1980) found that these young adults also lacked the skills to cope with stressful interpersonal interactions.

The Need for New Programs and New Approaches

In addition to using mental health services inappropriately, the young adults with mental illness had difficulty maintaining employment. Anthony (1979), Collingwood (1972), and Pierce and Drasgow (1969) identified obtaining and maintaining employment as a primary problem facing these young adults. Less than 25% of young adults with mental illness were able to maintain any type of competitive employment. Although some had once held jobs, most were unable to do so after the onset of their mental illness (Caton, 1981; Fine, 1980).

In the NAMI study (Unger & Anthony, 1984) discussed previously, 84% of the young adults were not working. However, their inability to work did not appear to be a result of their lack of intellectual ability or lack of education. (The parents in this study reported that 91% of the young adults had finished high school, and 58% had some college education.) The problem appeared to be their lack of work or career development skills and problems in social functioning.

The Department of Vocational Rehabilitation (DVR) is the federally funded agency that is responsible for providing vocational services to people with psychiatric disabilities. However, not only did the DVR not have the programs or resources at that time to meet this responsibility, but it also was often reluctant to work with these young adults because of the historically low rate of successful work placement for people with psychiatric disabilities.

Anthony, Howell, and Danley (1984) described the complexities of providing vocational services for a successful placement and found that adjusting successfully to a work environment did not correlate to adjusting to other environments. Individuals often lost their jobs because of their interpersonal skills—not because they lacked the ability to do the job. When these individuals did lose their jobs, however, they did not have the skills to find new jobs or to develop new vocational goals. Anthony et al. (1984) also found that individuals with mental illness had difficulty with transferring the skills they had learned in the hospital vocational programs to competitive work environments. Disincentives to working, which included the loss of Social Security benefits, Medicaid, and food stamps, also were important considerations. Because it was becoming increasingly clear that the old programs were not working and that a new approach was needed, a number of mental health agencies throughout the United States developed new programs specifically for young adults with mental illness.

Rockland County Community Mental Health Center (Rockland County, New York) developed a partial hospitalization program for young adults that included an acute stabilization component as an alternative to hospitalization, an intensive day treatment program, follow-up services, and a medication/monitoring clinic (Neffinger & Schiff, 1982). Dane County (Dane County, Wisconsin) developed a comprehensive program for young adults that included a 24-hour crisis intervention program, a day treatment program, cooperative apartments, medication clinics, support groups, and an outpatient therapy clinic (Stein & Test, 1982).

The Community Connection Program at St. Elizabeth's Hospital (Washington, D.C.) served as a model deinstitutionalization project for young adults (Harris & Bergman, 1984). The program used a psychosocial approach and an active focus on community involvement.

Reported results included that one third of the participants pursued vocational and educational goals, ranging from sheltered workshops to competitive employment. Psychosocial rehabilitation, as an intervention different from most treatment strategies, was just beginning. *Psychosocial rehabilitation programs* were designed to help people with mental illness explore and develop social, occupational, leisure, and living skills that would assist them to live as independently as possible in the community (Chambers, 1993).

Early Skills Training Programs

In spite of the special efforts discussed in the previous section, there were few programs generally available for young adults with mental illness. Most often it was business as usual: Day treatment programs provided a place in which to spend time but not in which to learn the vocational, educational, and social services that young adults needed. Although the treatment young adults received in the mental health centers may have been helpful in reducing symptomatology, it did not teach them the skills and competencies needed to function effectively in the community. In addition, the day treatment settings were perceived by young adults as too stigmatizing. The time was ripe for innovative programs in alternative settings.

At that time, an accumulating body of research evidence began to suggest that teaching people social and vocational skills could improve their functioning in the community. Reviews of literature showed that people with psychiatric disabilities could learn a variety of skills, regardless of their symptomatology (Anthony, 1979; Anthony, Cohen, & Cohen, 1978). Carkhuff (1972), Hersen and Bellack (1976), and Paul and Levitz (1977) reasoned that skills training for people with psychiatric disabilities was the preferred mode of intervention. Numerous authors described strategies that were designed to improve physical skills and physical fitness or to assist with personal hygiene; cooking; or using public transportation, recreational facilities, job tools, and physical fitness (Dodson & Mullens, 1969; Scoles & Fine, 1979; Shean, 1973; Stein, Test, & Marx, 1979).

Training programs were also designed to increase the young adults' skills in the emotional and interpersonal areas of functioning. Positive results were documented in the following skill areas: interpersonal (Hinterkopf & Brunswick, 1975), socialization (Hersen & Bellack, 1976), self-control (Cheek & Mendelson, 1975), problem solving (Coche & Flick, 1975), and job interviewing (Prazak, 1979).

Training in the area of intellectual functioning also helped to increase the skills of individuals with psychiatric disabilities in several areas, including managing money (Weinman, Sanders, Kleiner, & Wilson, 1970), seeking employment (McClure, 1973), and applying for jobs (Safieri, 1970). When these skills were properly integrated into a rehabilitation program that supported the use of these skills, the programs were able to have a significant impact on the individual's quality of life in the community (Anthony, 1979; Anthony & Margules, 1974).

Various researchers began to suggest that in order to provide the most typical experience possible, this educational and/or skills teaching intervention could be carried out in a non–mental health setting (Hefner & Gill, 1981; Lamb, 1976; Unger & Anthony, 1984). It was suggested that the college setting would be the ideal educational setting in which to initiate these interventions.

Programs Developed in Educational Settings

Mental health practitioners have hypothesized that in order for skills training to be most effective, it must be offered in a setting that young adults would view as nonstigmatizing and thus would attend regularly. In the mid-1970s, Lamb (1976) developed a skills-training program called Personal Growth Education, which was conducted in an academic setting. In this program, the individuals with psychiatric disabilities became students, and their problems in becoming part of their communities were viewed as skill limitations that were capable of being overcome through skills training. It was a radical departure from the belief that the individuals' problems were a result of their personalities, motivations, and upbringing and were amenable only to insight therapy. The educational environment also provided a normalized nonstigmatizing setting in which skills training could occur. The program was held at San Mateo Union High School (San Mateo, California) as part of an adult education program. Although it was not formally evaluated, positive results were reported.

A similar program was developed by Hefner and Gill (1981). The purpose of this program was to provide students with individualized skills-training courses through which career goals could be established and pursued. Prevocational, cognitively oriented vocational courses and vocational skills training courses were offered. The program, offered at the Reading Area Community College (Reading, Pennsylvania), was three semesters long, with the final semester focusing on supervised work experience. Positive results were reported in vocational outcomes.

Several other programs in academic settings were also being developed at that time. The La Guardia Transitional-Mental Health Worker Project at La Guardia Community College (La Guardia, New York) was developed to test whether individuals with prior psychiatric difficulties could be trained to function as mental health workers. Students in the program were enrolled in standard human services courses and were provided with personal support. Follow-up data reported favorable results when the students were compared with other human services students (Stein, 1981). Another program, located at George Brown College (Toronto, Ontario, Canada), focused on teaching community living skills. This program had a large enrollment and reported positive results (C. Schwengen, personal communication, November 22, 1981).

Based on the need to provide relevant services for a new and expanding group of individuals, the challenge for these early programs was to develop a program that would provide these individuals with vocational and social skills, improve their ability to live independently in the community, help them develop a reason to stay healthy, and create services for them that were nonstigmatizing and age appropriate. These early programs laid the groundwork for what was to become supported education. As the research was beginning to demonstrate in the early 1980s, individuals with a history of mental illness could learn skills and improve their functioning. The educational setting made sense in that it was both age appropriate and "normal."

The Continuing Education Program

In 1981, The Research and Training Center for Psychiatric Rehabilitation at Boston University (BU), as part of a larger grant, was funded by NIMH and the National Institute of Disability and Rehabilitation Research (NIDRR) to develop a rehabilitation program for young adults with mental illness. The program was designed to teach young adults the skills they would need to obtain employment, gain additional education, or acquire training that would lead to employment. The program was located in a classroom on the BU campus and was called the Continuing Education Program (CEP) (Unger et al., 1987).

Students who were enrolled in the CEP attended specially designed continuing education classes three times per week, for 2½ hours per day, and for four semesters. After completing the coursework, students were encouraged to stay connected with the CEP for support as they transferred to other colleges or universities or entered the workforce. Of the 52 students who participated, 35 completed the entire program (Unger, Anthony, Sciarappa, & Rogers, 1991). Outcomes of the study included the following: After the intervention, 42% of the students were competitively employed or enrolled in an education program (compared with 19% before the intervention), the number of hospitalizations experienced by the students significantly decreased, and their self-esteem significantly increased (Unger at al., 1991). Based on these outcomes, it seemed that an educational intervention at a post-secondary level warranted further attention.

The California Community College System Task Force

As young adults who had been diagnosed with mental illness began to return to school on their own, they began to attract the attention of many colleges. Although these individuals had been on campus before, their large numbers prompted the California Community College System to develop a task force to look at the implications for their college system. It was widely believed that this group of students was too ill, too disruptive, too unmotivated, or too academically unprepared to be successful in the role of college student (Parton, 1992). It was also thought that these students' needs were psychotherapeutic and, therefore, not within the purview of the community colleges.

To clearly define the issues and identify the problems, the California Community College System Task Force developed a systems approach to evaluate the needs of these students. The systems approach included educational support services, special instruction, and crisis intervention services (Parton, Amada, & Unger, 1991). The Task Force found that the standard educational support services provided to other students with disabilities through the Disabled Student Programs and Services (DSP&S) were appropriate and adequate for the majority of students with psychiatric disabilities. The Task Force also found that the DSP&S counselors' skills for assessing and providing educational supports were adequate for helping students with psychiatric disabilities, and, as a result, consultation from these mental health professionals was made available.

The Task Force found that students who requested educational accommodations and services were, in fact, qualified to receive them based on DSP&S guidelines. The students seldom requested services that were considered inappropriate, and the crisis services that had been put in place for them were underutilized. The study further showed that, as a group, the students with psychiatric disabilities were not disruptive on campus.

All of the previously discussed events—the emergence of a special group of young adults with mental illness, the lack of effective programs to support this group of individuals, the initial efforts to use skills teaching as a mental health intervention, and providing services in an educational setting—laid the foundation for the development of supported education. These first research and demonstration projects, the CEP at BU and the work of the California Community College System Task Force and its model programs, provided the information to justify further exploration of how this newly identified resource could be defined and expanded so that its potential could be realized. The next step was to expand the number of service sites.

Disseminating Supported Education

The initial efforts to develop programs that would help young adults with mental illness return to college were well received by the young adults, their parents, the mental health providers, and many post-secondary schools. However, money was not widely available to develop these new programs. (The initial programs had been funded by grants.) To address this issue, the Center for Psychiatric Rehabilitation was awarded a 5-year grant to disseminate the concept of supported education and to develop pilot projects that did not require any extra funds. The goal was to utilize existing resources to provide this service.

Seven sites throughout the United States were identified (Unger, 1993). Each site had demonstrated a commitment to providing services to young adults and had begun the process of developing relationships with related community agencies. The Center for Psychiatric Rehabilitation was to provide consultation and evaluation services. In order to be as inclusive as possible and to explore a variety of program sites, different kinds of service agencies/institutions were included in the project. The sites chosen were a publicly funded psychiatric hospital, a psychiatric hospital in collaboration with a university, a mental health association, a vocational technical institute, a county mental health system, and two community colleges.

All of the sites were committed to the values of supported education (see "Program Values" section) and implemented their programs by reordering service priorities, reallocating resources, and reassigning staff members. Rather than finding new money, existing resources were utilized. This reallocation was carried out in the mental health setting by changing priorities, eliminating programs to put resources into the supported education program, or reassigning staff time so that a staff position could be allocated for the new program. In the educational setting, the definition of the service population was expanded by the Disability Services (DS) Offices to include students with psychiatric disabilities as well as those with physical and learning disabilities.

Networks and coalitions were developed within the provider community so that college and mental health centers could work together in both the planning and implementation of these new services. Agencies and organizations that were involved in the local communities included local chapters of the NAMI; consumer groups; Vocational Rehabilitation; mental health associations; housing, mental health, and psychiatric hospitals; and educational institutions, most notably community colleges. At one site, an advisory board representing the various constituencies was developed; at another, a permanent community coalition that continued to meet to plan for both the mental health and education needs of their county was developed (Unger, 1993).

The successful implementation of the dissemination project fortified the notion that helping young adults with mental illness to enroll or to return to postsecondary education was a viable option in service delivery. As the ideas and various program models were disseminated, supported education programs were added to the services traditionally delivered by mental health agencies. Many colleges and universities opened their doors and expanded their services to include students with psychiatric disabilities. As the programs developed, a theoretical foundation with a definition of supported education and underlying values emerged.

THEORETICAL PERSPECTIVE OF SUPPORTED EDUCATION

Helping people with a history of mental illness to return to school was a radical departure from the medical model of curing an illness and providing insight therapy. This approach reflected other changes within the mental health field and represented a new approach to working with people with mental illness. This approach had begun its earlier development at what came to be known as psychosocial centers, such as Fountain House in New York City and Horizon House in Philadelphia, Pennsylvania. These centers were founded by groups of former patients for mutual aid and support. The concept of psychosocial rehabilitation was further articulated and developed by other centers such as Thresholds in Chicago, Illinois; the Social Center for Psychiatric Rehabilitation in Fairfax, Virginia; Center Club in Boston, Massachusetts; Fellowship House in Miami, Florida; Hill House in Cleveland, Ohio; and Portals House in Los Angeles, California (Anthony, Cohen, & Farkas, 1990).

Psychiatric Rehabilitation as a Foundation for Supported Education

The growth of psychosocial centers, in combination with the funding of a research and training center at BU and the funding for the development, study, and dissemination of psychiatric rehabilitation (a particular kind of psychosocial rehabilitation), continued the articulation and implementation of a rehabilitation approach. The rehabilitation approach used in psychiatric rehabilitation modeled itself on the tenets of physical rehabilitation. Unlike treatment, which was based on the sickness–wellness dichotomy or on the medical model, psychiatric rehabilitation was based more on a physical rehabilitation model that examined the skills and supports necessary for the individual to function in a particular environment (Anthony, 1979). Rather than trying to "cure" an individual, improved functioning was the goal.

To facilitate improved functioning and to meet the goals of the individual, assessments were conducted to determine the skills that the individual would need to be successful in a particular environment. Assessments were also conducted to examine the supportive resources someone would need to improve his or her participation in a particular environment. For instance, in physical rehabilitation, an individual may need a wheelchair and a home health aid as support. He or she may need to learn certain skills in maneuvering a wheelchair or in transferring him- or herself from the wheelchair to a bed or to the bathtub. The individual also may need supportive counseling while making adjustments with ongoing support during the transition to more independent living.

Similarly, an individual with a psychiatric disability may need to learn new skills that help to manage the symptoms associated with his or her illness. The individual also may need skills to assess his or her career needs and goals. Many individuals need the support of Social Security, vocational rehabilitation services, or supportive counseling when they take on new tasks or move into new settings. Ongoing support in this realm can be useful as the individual continues to make changes in his or her life.

Similar to an individual with a physical disability requiring continued periodic medical attention and medication, an individual with a psychiatric disability may also require continued medical attention and medication. As with a chronic illness or physical disability, people with a psychiatric disability may have to return to the hospital periodically if their symptoms worsen. It is important that both treatment and rehabilitation occur together as they are needed.

Skill teaching and providing support are critical components of the psychiatric rehabilitation model, which emphasizes outcomes articulated by the individual rather than the rehabilitation process itself. Depending on the person's needs, treatment also may need to be ongoing. Another component of the psychiatric rehabilitation model is the importance of a trusting relationship between the individual and the rehabilitation counselor or other team members. In this relationship, all rehabilitation efforts must come from the frame of reference of the individual and be developed in an atmosphere of hope and encouragement. The service provider's unconditional positive regard and nonjudgmental listening are essential.

These three components—skill instruction, providing support, and a trusting relationship with the provider—became the components of psychiatric rehabilitation. This approach, particularly with its orientation on outcomes, was utilized to help individuals with mental illness return to work. It was with this rehabilitation philosophy and with its emphasis on outcome that the definition and values of supported education were drawn and articulated.

DEFINITION OF SUPPORTED EDUCATION

The definition of supported education is based on the definition of supported employment. The Rehabilitation Act Amendments of 1986 (PL 99-506) defined *supported employment* as

> Competitive work in integrated settings is (a) for individuals with severe handicaps for whom competitive employment has not traditionally occurred, or (b) for whom competitive employment has been interrupted or intermittent as a result of severe disability, and who, because of their handicap, need ongoing support services to perform such work.

Using this definition as a model, *supported education* is defined as

> Education in integrated settings for people with severe psychiatric disabilities for whom postsecondary education has not traditionally occurred or for people for whom postsecondary education has been interrupted or intermittent as a result of a severe psychiatric disability, and who, because of their handicap, need ongoing support services to be successful in the education environment. (Unger, 1990, p. 10)

A number of programs that met the definition of supported education began to emerge in the 1980s. These programs represented different approaches to providing services to young adults in the college setting. The approaches fell into three prototypes: self-contained classroom, on-site support, and mobile support. The prototypes were evaluated by two characteristics: 1) the level of integration of the program into the school site and 2) where the support was provided. The following is a brief overview of each supported education prototype (Unger, 1990).

Self-Contained Classroom

In the self-contained classroom prototype, students attend classes on a postsecondary site in a self-contained classroom with other students who have psychiatric disabilities. The curriculum is set, and all students receive the same instruction in the same classroom. The students are not initially integrated into general education classes, but they may participate in all of the institution's activities and use the institution's re-sources. However, support is available from program staff for students as they progress and move into general classes. Program staff may be from the sponsoring program and/or the academic institution. For ex-ample, the CEP at BU was a four-semester program in which staff from the Center for Psychiatric Rehabilitation taught career development skills at Sargent College on the BU campus.

On-Site Support

In the on-site support prototype, students attend general classes at the postsecondary site where they are matriculated and for which they re-ceive credit. Support is provided by staff from the postsecondary site through the DS Office or Mental Health/Counseling Services. For in-stance, the College of San Mateo provides a reentry class, which is taught by a faculty member for credit. At San Mateo, support is pro-vided by college staff. A variation of this model is when the support services or special classes are taught by a mental health services provider (rather than a faculty member) who has an office on campus.

Mobile Support

Similar to the on-site support model, in the mobile support prototype, students attend the colleges and classes of their choice. In this model, however, the support is provided by staff from community-based mental health services rather than from the college. Although these staff members are located at the community mental health services, they are available to provide support to the students on-site at a vari-ety of postsecondary institutions. Thresholds has a community schol-ars program that provides support to students as they attend many dif-ferent colleges, universities, and technical schools in the Chicago area.

CHARACTERISTICS OF SUPPORTED EDUCATION

Supported education can be further defined in terms of its philosophy, mission, values, and policies (Unger, 1990).

Program Philosophy

The primary philosophy on which supported education is based is psy-chosocial rehabilitation. However, supported education also draws heavily from both client-centered therapy and social learning theory.

In client-centered therapy (Rogers, 1951), there is an assumption that the movement made by the client to self-enhancement, self-consistency, and self-actualization is supported by the therapist believing in the worth and significance of the individual. This valuing of the person with which the therapist is working is expressed as unconditional positive regard (Rogers, 1951). Rogers believed that a certain type of faith or belief can achieve certain results. He said that "the individual has the capacity to deal constructively with all those aspects of his life which can potentially come into conscious awareness" (1951, p. 71). Although supported education practitioners do not try to develop therapeutic relationships with their students, they do attempt to help and support. In essence, the same practices and beliefs expressed by Rogers—primarily unconditional positive regard—are fundamental to developing and maintaining a collaborative, helping relationship with the students.

Historically, people with mental illness were not seen as capable of changing their behaviors, making important decisions about their lives, or having the same value systems as others. The attitudes of the mental health practitioners and the treatment that they provided were often paternalistic and condescending. As changes in the mental health system and its practitioners occurred, emphasis on client-centered interactions or, in the case of supported education, student-centered interactions became very important. Unconditional positive regard, respect for the individual, and belief that the individual can learn and honor what he or she has experienced with the mental illness is necessary for these students to achieve their potential.

These practices are further supported by social learning theory (Rotter, 1976). Social learning theory states that "the study of the personality is the study of learned behavior. Learned behavior is modifiable; it changes with experience" (Rotter, 1976, p. 84). This concept also is elemental to supported education; however, social learning theory adds two critical elements to its theoretical perspective: 1) the belief that the person can change through learning by experience and 2) the emphasis on the meaningfulness of the environment. Rotter said that "major or basic modes of behaving are learned in social situations" (1976, p. 84).

Attending classes, interacting with other students and college staff, and fulfilling an educational or vocational goal all provide many new learning experiences. The college setting is for most people a meaningful environment. The payoffs or satisfactions are high for those who fit in and are successful. The demands are quite different from those in a mental health treatment program or a psychiatric hospital, and the rewards are often more desirable. The college campus provides great motivation for people to learn or relearn functional behaviors and to change old, dysfunctional behaviors.

In summary, the philosophy of supported education is based on three major schools of thought:

1. The psychiatric rehabilitation approach, which emphasizes the teaching of skills and providing the needed supports within the context of a helping relationship
2. Client-centered therapy, which provides unconditional positive regard to the student and the belief that there is a natural movement toward health
3. The social learning theory, which states that learned behavior can change with experience and that the environment provides a meaningful and important setting for learning to occur

Program Mission

The mission of supported education is similar to that of most colleges and universities: to provide educational services to the community. However, an additional emphasis is placed on improved opportunities to gain access to and increased retention of people with psychiatric disabilities. For example, a supported education program's mission statement might read as follows: to provide educational and support services to people with psychiatric disabilities in a postsecondary setting so that they can have access to and successfully utilize the educational environment.

Program Values

Program values are the underlying beliefs that govern all actions related to program development and service delivery. They also give substance to the underlying philosophy of supported education. The following values clarify and concretize the philosophy of supported education.

- *Support:* Services that the student perceives to be supportive should be provided as long as they are needed.
- *Normalization:* Services should be culturally normative and use nonstigmatizing methods and settings. Services should be integrated or generally consistent with the typical routines of life within the postsecondary environment.
- *Availability and accessibility:* The institution's programs and services should be publicized to current and prospective students so that

they can use the services, which should be located on campus at a convenient location.

- *Individualized services:* The services should be tailored to meet the unique and changing needs of each student.
- *Dignity:* Services should be provided in a manner and in an environment that protects individuals' privacy and enhances their personal dignity.
- *Self-determination:* Students should retain the fullest possible control of their own lives. This means that they are the ones to set their goals and participate fully in determining the criteria for success and in evaluating their progress toward meeting their goals.
- *Indefinite duration:* Services should be available for as long as students need and/or want such support.
- *Flexibility:* Services are evaluated on an ongoing basis so that they can be revised as needed to keep them responsive to student needs.
- *Coordination:* The resources of the educational setting and the resources in the community should be brought together to work for the benefit of the students.
- *Hope:* Students are treated as developing individuals who are capable of growth and positive change (Unger, 1993).

Program Policies

Entry criteria for a college generally includes two elements: 1) an age limit and 2) some reference to academic potential. There is usually a minimum age limit (often 18 years of age). Academic criteria, depending on the educational setting, may range from high academic standards to being able to benefit from the instructional programs of the educational institution. Based on these common requirements, entry criteria for determining the appropriateness of a student for supported education may include the following:

- Written verification of psychological disability diagnosed by a licensed mental health professional (for funding purposes)
- Ability to meet the educational admission and retention standards
- Ability to meet the minimum age requirements and to benefit from the instructional programs in an educational setting if supported education services are provided
- Ability to complete the necessary admission and matriculation processes
- Not currently an imminent danger to him- or herself or to others
- Appropriate behavior during the admissions interview (i.e., the individual acts in a manner appropriate to the intake process and ap-

pears to be able to provide informed consent regarding service provision policies and the educational institution's code of conduct).
* Expressed willingness to use supported education services

The historical changes in the mental health treatment process and the large numbers of young adults entering the system have opened the door for new thinking to emerge. The development of a theoretical perspective provided a base on which new programs could be built.

THE PURPOSE OF SUPPORTED EDUCATION

The purpose of a supported education program is to improve access to college and to increase retention of people who have a history of mental illness. The primary goal is to assist them, as members of the community, to fully utilize this valuable resource.

The college or university is not a treatment setting nor is a supported education program a treatment program. Treatment is the role of the mental health system; education is the role of the postsecondary education site. As part of their education mandate, however, colleges and universities must provide accommodations so that their requirements do not discriminate against people with disabilities.

Many colleges also provide additional support services to help students with disabilities complete their programs. Some colleges go a step further and have programs designed for people with psychiatric disabilities that are similar to the programs designed for other groups of individuals on the campus. Supported education programs may also exist as part of a constellation of services offered by mental health agencies. Supported education services for students can be strengthened when there is collaboration and cooperation between colleges and mental health agencies.

SUMMARY

During the mid-1980s, young adults who were diagnosed with mental illnesses did not require lengthy hospitalizations because of new medications. However, they did not want to be identified with the older individuals who were labeled "chronically mentally ill," and they often refused to use the same community services as the older individuals. It is these young adults who prompted the development of supported education programs, and it is these people for whom and about whom this book is written.

Supported education is a concept grounded in rehabilitation theory, which states that although people with a mental illness may have a psychiatric disability, every individual—regardless of his or her symptoms—can improve. Although medical interventions may be critical to treating mental illness, rehabilitation is also critical to improving the functioning of individuals with this diagnosis. With unconditional positive regard and the understanding of the importance of learning new behaviors in the environment, many people with a mental illness have found new meaning and productivity by returning to college.

REFERENCES

Anthony, W.A. (1979). *The principles of psychiatric rehabilitation.* Baltimore: University Park Press.

Anthony, W.A., Buell, G., Sharratt, S., & Althoff, M. (1972). Efficacy of psychiatric rehabilitation. *Psychological Bulletin, 87*(6), 447–456.

Anthony, W.A., Cohen, M., & Cohen B. (1978). The chronic mental patient: Five years later. In J. Talbot (Ed.), *Psychiatric rehabilitation* (pp. 137–157). New York: Grune & Stratton.

Anthony, W.A., Cohen, M., & Farkas, M. (1990). *Psychiatric rehabilitation.* Boston: Boston University Center for Psychiatric Rehabilitation.

Anthony, W.A., & Margules, A. (1974). Toward improving the efficacy of psychiatric rehabilitation: A skills training approach. *Rehabilitation Psychology, 21,* 101–105.

Anthony, Howell, & Danley. (1984). Vocational rehabilitation of the psychiatrically disabled. In M. Mirabi (Ed.), *The chronically mentally ill: Research and services* (pp. 215–237). Jamaica, NY: Medical and Scientific Books.

Bachrach, L.L. (1982a). Program planning for young adult chronic patients. In B. Pepper & H. Ryglewicz (Eds.), *The young adult chronic patient revisited: New directions for mental health services sourcebook* (pp. 99–109). San Francisco: Jossey-Bass.

Bachrach, L.L. (1982b). Young adult chronic patients: An analytical review of the literature. *Hospital and Community Psychiatry, 33,* 189–197.

Bassuk, E. (1980). The impact of deinstitutionalization of the general hospital psychiatric emergency ward. *Hospital and Community Psychiatry, 30,* 623–627.

Carkhuff, R.R. (1972). *Helping and human relations* (Vols. 1–2). New York: Holt, Rinehart & Winston.

Caton, C.L. (1981). The new chronic patient and the system of community care. *Hospital and Community Psychiatry, 32*(7), 475–478.

Chambers, C. (1993). Editorial. *Psychosocial Rehabilitation Journal, 16*(3), 1.

Cheek, F.E., & Mendelson, M. (1975). Developing behavior modification programs with an emphasis on self-control. *Hospital and Community Psychiatry, 24,* 410–416.

Coche, E., & Flick, A. (1975). Problem solving training groups for hospitalized patients. *The Journal of Psychology, 91,* 19–29.

Collingwood, T. (1972). Effects of physical training upon behavior and self attitudes. *Journal of Clinical Psychology, 28,* 583–585.

Dodson, L.C., & Mullens, W.R. (1969). Some effects of jogging on psychiatric hospital patients. *American Corrective Therapy Journal, 23,* 130–134.

Egri, G., & Caton, C.L. (1981). *Serving the young adult chronic patient in the 1980's:*

Challenge to the general hospital. Paper presented at the American Association for General Hospital Psychiatry, San Diego, CA.

Fine, S.B. (1980). Psychiatric treatment and rehabilitation: What's in a name? *Journal of the National Association of Private Psychiatric Hospitals, 11*(5), 8–13.

Goldman, A., Gattozzi, C., & Yawke, D. (1981). Defining and counting the chronically mentally ill. *Hospital and Community Psychiatry, 32*(2), 21–27.

Harris, M., & Bergman, H.C. (1984). The young adult chronic patient: Affective responses to treatment. In B. Pepper & H. Ryglewicz (Eds.), *The young adult chronic patient revisited: New Directions for mental health services sourcebook* (pp. 29–37). San Francisco: Jossey Bass.

Hefner, F., & Gill, R. (1981). *The role of community based service providers in the rehabilitation of deinstitutionalized psychiatric patients: Does education belong in the therapeutic process?* Unpublished manuscript.

Hersen, M., & Bellack, A. (1976). Social skills for chronic psychiatric patients: Rationale, research, findings and further directions. *Comprehensive Psychiatry, 17,* 559–580.

Hinterkopf, E., & Brunswick, L.K. (1975). Teaching therapeutic skills to mental patients. *Psychotherapy: Theory, Research and Practice, 12,* 8–12.

Lamb, H.R. (1976). An educational model for teaching living skills to long-term patients. *Hospital and Community Psychiatry, 27*(12), 875–877.

McClure, D.P. (1973). Placement through improvement of client's job-seeking skills. *Journal of Applied Rehabilitation Counseling, 3,* 188–196.

National Institute of Mental Health (NIMH). (1980). *Announcement of community support system strategy development and implementation grants.* Rockville, MD: Author.

National Institute of Mental Health (NIMH), Division of Biometry and Epidemiology. (1977, June 27). *Resident patient rate in state mental hospitals reduced to one-fourth the 1955 rate* [Memorandum No. 6.] Rockville, MD: Author.

Neffinger, J., & Schiff, J.W. (1982). Treatment by objectives: A partial hospital treatment program. In B. Pepper & H. Ryglewicz (Eds.), *The young adult chronic patient revisited: New directions for mental health services sourcebook* (pp. 77–84). San Francisco: Jossey-Bass.

Pandiani, J., & Butterfield, C. (1980, November). Client profiles and conditions on termination of clients served by community mental health centers in Central Vermont, Washington County Mental Health Services, Montpelier.

Parton, D.G. (1992). *Model service sites for students with psychological disabilities.* Sacramento, CA: Chancellor's Office, Student Services Division, Disabled Student Programs and Services (DSP&S) Unit.

Parton, D.G., Amada, G., & Unger, K.V. (1991). *Components of a systems approach: Resource guide for serving students with psychological disabilities in California Community Colleges.* Sacramento, CA: Chancellor's Office, Student Services Division, DSP&S Unit.

Paul, F., & Levitz, R. (1977). *The psychosocial treatment of chronic mental patients.* Cambridge, MA: Harvard University Press.

Pepper B., & Ryglewicz, H. (1984).Treating the young adult chronic patient: An update. In B. Pepper & H. Ryglewicz (Eds.), *The young adult chronic patient revisited: New directions for mental health services sourcebook* (pp. 5–15). San Francisco: Jossey-Bass.

Pierce, R.M., & Drasgow, J. (1969). Teaching facilitative interpersonal functioning to psychiatric patients. *Journal of Counseling Psychology, 16,* 295–298.

Prazak, J.A. (1979). Learning job-seeking interview skills. In Krumboltz & Thoreson (Eds.), *Behavioral counseling*. New York: Holt, Rinehart & Winston.

Rehabilitation Act Amendments of 1986, PL 99-506, 29 U.S.C., §§ 701 *et seq.*

Rogers, C. (1951). *Client-centered therapy: Its current practice, implications and theory*. Boston: Houghton Mifflin.

Rotter, J. (1976). *Social learning theory and clinical psychology*. New York: Johnson Reprint Corp.

Safieri, D. (1970). Using an education model in a sheltered workshop program. *Mental Hygiene, 54*, 140–143.

Scoles, P., & Fine, E. (1979). Aftercare and rehabilitation in a community mental health center. *Social Work, 16*, 75–82.

Shean, G. (1973). An effective and self-supporting program of community living for chronic patients. *Hospital and Community Psychiatry, 24*, 97–99.

Stein, E. (1981). Report from La Guardia: Transitional mental health worker project. *Federation of Parents for the New York State Mental Institutions, Inc.,* 14–16.

Stein, L.I., & Test, M.A. (1982). Community treatment of the young adult patient. In B. Pepper & H. Ryglewicz (Ed.), *The young adult chronic patient revisited: New directions for mental health services sourcebook* (pp. 57–67). San Francisco: Jossey-Bass.

Stein, L.I., Test, M.A., & Marx, A.J. (1979). Alternatives to the hospital: A controlled study. *American Journal of Psychiatry, 132*, 517–522.

Unger, K. (1987). Rehabilitation through education: A university-based continuing education program for young adults with psychiatric disabilities (Doctoral dissertation. Boston University, 1986). *Dissertation Abstracts International, 47A*(11), p. 4060.

Unger, K. (1990, Summer). Supported postsecondary education for people with mental illness. *American Rehabilitation*, 10–14.

Unger, K. (1993). Creating supported education programs utilizing existing community resources. *Psychosocial Rehabilitation Journal, 17*(1), 11–23.

Unger, K., & Anthony, W. (1984). Are families satisfied with services to young adult chronic patients? A recent survey and a proposed alternative. In B. Pepper & H. Ryglewicz (Eds.), *The young adult chronic patient revisited: New directions for mental health services sourcebook* (pp. 91–98). San Francisco: Jossey-Bass.

Unger, K., Anthony, W., Sciarappa, K., & Rogers, E.S. (1991). Development and evaluation of a supported education for young adults with long-term mental illness. *Hospital and Community Psychiatry, 42*(8), 838–842.

Wagner, B.A. (1981). *Progress report: Community support programs for the long-term mentally ill in Wisconsin*. Madison: Wisconsin Bureau of Mental Health.

Wallace, C., Nelson, C., Liberman, R., Aitchison, R., Lukoff, D., Elder, J., & Ferris, C. (1980). A review and critique for social skills training with schizophrenic patients. *Schizophrenia Bulletin, 6*(1), 42–63.

Weinman, B., Sanders, R., Kleiner, R., & Wilson, S. (1970). Community based treatment of the chronic psychotic. *Community Mental Health Journal, 6*, 12–21.

2

Understanding
Mental Disorders

*He was the third of four children, well accepted by his siblings, a
wanted child by his parents, bright, full of insatiable curiosity.
He started school at Hebrew Academy but had to be withdrawn
early, having trouble with the Hebrew language. In public school
he had trouble with the English language. He read faster back-
wards than others read forward ("was" became "saw," "pin" was
"nip"). After much trial and error he was diagnosed as having
moderate dyslexia, a learning disability, and thereafter his mother
patiently explained his difficulty yearly to his new teachers.*

*His grades were good; he was accepted by playmate peers. And,
in private school, at age 12, he developed an interest in science,
physics in particular. Math, Calculus, Physics—all facets were
readily and quickly grasped. A's only. The best grades of all four
children. Accepted by a prestigious Eastern school, he seemed to
adjust until his third year, when it all fell apart.*

*He would lie in bed until noon. Stopped attending to his per-
sonal needs. Read only the Bible. Had visions and conversations
with God. At times thought he was Jesus, Allah, Buddha. His
"voices" told him what to do and encompassed his total behavior.
He could hold no conversation; would not respond. He grew a
long scraggly beard and walked the campus carrying a seven foot
wooden staff. Picked up by the police, parents notified, withdrawn
from college, he secluded himself in his room at home; finally the
diagnosis . . . paranoid schizophrenia. (Jaffe, 1993, pp. 61–62)*

23

*Everyone, in and out of the hospital, asks me what Robert's diag-
nosis is, and why I think it is Robert broke this time and what I
think precipitated the break? The questions—with the years, and
with the repeated breakdowns and hospitalizations—seem absurd.
Whatever the immediate causes, the ultimate causes (and answers)
seem obvious: because of his life. (Neugeboren, 1997, p. 128)*

The onset of a major mental illness often occurs between the ages of
18 and 25, a time when young people are just beginning to prepare
themselves for adulthood. Most young adults during these years have
begun to work, are preparing for a career, or are enrolled in college. As
they approach the end of their teens and early 20s, they have many
other developmental tasks to master in addition to career development. These tasks include preparing for family life, achieving emotional independence from parents and other adults, acquiring a code of
ethics, and learning socially responsible behavior (Havighurst, 1972).
Similar to all developmental tasks, there is an optimal time for mastery
for each one of these milestones (Erikson, 1963). After that critical win-
dow of time has passed, the mastery becomes more difficult.

Young adults with a mental illness who are unable to get immediate treatment and appropriate care for their illness or who do not respond to the care that is provided may find themselves developmen-
tally behind their peers. One student remarked,

> While you were out there dating and having fun, working part-time jobs
> and learning the hundreds of things that make your life easier now, I was
> in the hospital or so depressed I couldn't get out of bed. No wonder I'm
> behind! (Anonymous student, cited in Unger, 1997)

Many of these young adults end up feeling socially awkward and
ill prepared, both interpersonally and vocationally, to begin a career or
a family. The stigma and misconceptions attached to mental illness
may also limit the opportunities available for a young adult to experi-
ment and learn in an appropriate and accepting environment. With the
onset of a mental illness, the development of the brain may itself also
be affected.

Neuroimaging advances, including computed tomography, mag-
netic resonance imaging, and positron emission tomography scans are
beginning to show that the areas of the brain affected by a mental illness also may be the areas that are critical to many aspects of personality functioning, including the ability to plan, to problem solve, and to

modulate impulsive and inappropriate behavior (Wirshing, 1991). The increased knowledge of brain chemistry and functioning has changed our understanding of mental illness. It is widely believed that what has been called a *mental illness* may in fact be a neurobiological disorder. The neuroimaging advances reveal "reproducible, scientifically verifiable abnormalities in brain anatomy, chemistry, and function that help explain the serious brain disorders affecting a human being's cognition, emotions, and behaviors" (Peschel & Peschel, 1991, p. 4). Peschel and Peschel stated that

> The revolution occurring in neurobiology and molecular biology has documented that serious mental illnesses are, in fact, physical illnesses characterized by, or resulting from, malfunctions and/or malformations of the brain. Among these physical illnesses are schizophrenia, schizo-affective disorder, bipolar and major depressive disorders, autism, pervasive developmental disorders, obsessive-compulsive disorders, Tourette's disorder, anxiety and panic disorders, and attention deficit hyperactivity disorder. (1991, p. 4)

THE CONCEPT OF MENTAL ILLNESS

The concept of mental illness as a brain dysfunction is not universally accepted. Many mental health practitioners and consumers attribute the causes of a mental disorder to life experiences, such as severe and persistent abuse, marginalization, or spiritual emergencies. Penney (in press) summarized four models that have emerged from the consumer/survivor/ex-patient movement literature. They provide alternative ways of understanding and responding to mental illness and are substantially different from the medical model that was previously described. The alternative models emphasize wellness and recovery rather than illness.

The Disability Model

The disability model has its origin in the physical disability movement and is based on the belief that injury, trauma, or other conditions can affect a person's ability to function in certain ways. A disability is seen not as an illness but as a condition that can be compensated for with the use of accommodations.

The Social/Economic/Political Model

The social/economic/political model is based on the belief that mental and emotional distress is primarily a result of the conditions in which people are living or in which they have been raised. Potential causative factors include poverty, racial and gender discrimination, physical and emotional trauma, and marginalization.

The Spiritual Model

The spiritual model is based on the belief that mental and emotional distress is essentially spiritual in nature. Symptoms are seen as spiritual imbalances or changes associated with spiritual growth. Psychosis is an extreme but fully human experience that can be managed by paying attention to spiritual discipline and growth.

The Recovery Model

The recovery model is based on the belief that people can and do recover from a mental illness rather than on the actual cause of the mental illness. Various methods, many of which are nonmedical, are used for recovery, including self-help, mutual support, self-determination, and choice.

MISUNDERSTANDING MENTAL ILLNESS

Over an extended period of time, the various models discussed in the previous section may become part of an integrated picture that allows for individual differences, causes, and beliefs. However, even though the understanding of how the brain functions has improved and new ways have emerged to describe mental illness, there is still much misunderstanding about mental illness and the people who have this diagnosis.

Myths and Realities
About People with Mental Illness

As people with mental illness continue to receive treatment in their communities rather than having long-term stays in psychiatric hospitals, as research on the most effective treatment for mental illness continues, and as new psychotropic medications for treating mental illness are developed, knowledge, attitudes, and beliefs about mental illness continue to change. Many things that were believed to be true in the past have been proven false or are being changed through increased knowledge and experience. Many myths are being dispelled. Some of the myths are listed in the following subsections along with the new understanding and knowledge, particularly related to postsecondary education.

Myth #1: When most of us think of people with a mental disorder, the stigma of mental illness arises. Images of dirty, homeless people talking to themselves or headlines about mass murders and bizarre crimes come to mind. Although homelessness, particularly in major cities, is a reality and criminal acts are sensationalized, we tend to generalize these images to all people with mental illness.

Reality: People with mental illness have more similarities than differences with the general population. These individuals want the same things that everyone wants: a home, a family, a job, and a place in the community. Individuals with mental illness also want a standard of living that allows them to fulfill their basic human needs. People with mental illness do not commit more crimes than the rest of the population (Monahan & Arnold, 1996). In fact, these individuals are more frequently the victims of crimes because they are so vulnerable.

Myth #2: Traditionally, mental illness was seen as a chronic, lifelong disease. When entering the hospital for the first time, many people were told that their lives were over and that they should never expect to raise a family, complete school, or get a good job.

Reality: Harding (1988) found that most people (50%–70%) do recover from schizophrenia. New medications and support services allow people with major depression or bipolar disorder to manage their illnesses sufficiently so that they can lead more rewarding lives. People diagnosed with an anxiety or personality disorder also improve with treatment. Many people who never expected to get out of the hospital are living successfully in the community. Few individuals need prolonged hospital stays or intensive care for long periods of time. The treatment of choice is to stabilize the symptoms in the hospital through medication and then provide the necessary treatment and support in the community. Many people who receive rehabilitation and supportive services do not need to be on medication for the rest of their lives.

Myth #3: Traditionally, people with psychiatric disabilities have been placed, through either the mental health system or the vocational rehabilitation system, in entry-level or dead-end jobs. It was believed that they could not manage the stress of demanding work.

Reality: Studies conducted in the 1990s have shown that with proper training and support, people with mental illness can work efficiently and effectively (Bond, Drake, Mueser, & Becker, 1997; Drake et al., 1994). In a 1997 study at the University of Arizona (Unger, 1997), approximately one quarter of the participants who held jobs were working full or part time in middle-management positions. As a result of the disincentives built into the Social Security system, however, many people with a mental illness are reluctant to work full time because if they do, they will lose their benefits.

Myth #4: Historically, it was believed that the nature of mental illness, defined as thought and mood disorders, prevented people from learning.

Reality: Since the 1970s, the practice of teaching skills (e.g., independent living skills) gained popularity as a method of intervention. This demonstrated that, in fact, people with mental illness could learn simple skills. This idea paved the way, over time, for the development of supported education. Although people with a mental illness may have greater difficulty with some learning, depending solely on the person's ability, symptoms, and motivation, their learning problems usually do not prevent them from achieving their educational goals.

Myth #5: It was believed that people with mental illness would cause problems and disrupt the learning environment if they returned to school. As a result, many school administrators were reluctant to have people with a known psychiatric disability on their campuses.

Reality: In a study conducted in the California Community College System (Parton, 1993), students with a known psychiatric disability were not the students on campus causing the problems. This finding has also been supported by many education programs around the United States. However, the standard practice has become that should students with a mental illness cause problems on campus, they are responsible to the same code of student conduct that all students are and treated accordingly.

Myth #6: Many psychiatrists and mental health services providers believed that going back to school would be too stressful for their clients. This attitude was also shared by many potential students and their families.

Reality: With proper support and symptom management, people with mental illness are able to take on the challenges of more meaningful activities. It is important that medications be monitored to compensate for the added activities and demands. Many psychiatrists have seen improvement in their patients as their patients start school and, consequently, decrease their medication dosages. However, this often leads to a relapse during midterm exams and as students respond to the stress of papers that are due and other exams that are scheduled. Students may need more medication—rather than less—during these times.

Myth #7: Many school personnel believed that students with a psychiatric disability would require more resources and time than other students with disabilities.

Reality: Many programs have found that students with psychiatric disabilities do need more time initially to register for classes, to apply for financial aid, or to receive academic counseling. They also may need more personal support. However, the amount of time that these students need decreases as they become acclimated to the campus environment and develop a support network. In general, students with mental illness do not put a disproportionate drain on a school's resources.

MAJOR MENTAL ILLNESSES

It is important to understand the nature of the major mental illnesses so that medical records can be used effectively for determining eligibility to receive accommodations and services from the disability services offices at different institutions. It is also helpful to understand why students may behave as they do at certain times. It is critical to understand that these categories of disorders are simply an attempt to make sense of a constellation of symptoms that may change over time, manifest themselves more at one time than another, overlap, and are different for each person. When someone receives a diagnosis, he or she does not "become" that diagnosis. For instance, having a diagnosis of schizophrenia does not make a person a schizophrenic; the diagnosis simply states that the person has symptoms that fall under this category of mental disorder in one labeling system. Each person is equal to more than his or her diagnosis, just as a person who has diabetes is more than a diabetic; he or she is also a family member, a worker, a friend, and so on.

The *Diagnostic and Statistical Manual of Mental Disorders, Fourth Edition* (DSM-IV) (American Psychiatric Association [APA], 1994) is the manual used most often by professionals in the mental health field to determine the diagnosis of mental illness. It is important to remember that the diagnosis, which lists descriptions of symptoms and behaviors, is not precise and is not always well defined. Doctors often disagree about which labels to use, and the DSM has been revised four times. In addition, there may be overlaps among several diagnoses. For example, an individual may concurrently be diagnosed as having symptoms of schizophrenia, major depression, and a personality disorder by one psychiatrist and a different constellation of diagnoses from another psychiatrist.

The descriptions of the most common diagnoses are summarized in the following subsections. The descriptions are not meant to be complete or definitive but instead are meant to give the reader a general idea of each diagnosis. All of the diagnoses described are Axis I diagnoses (i.e., considered to be clinical syndromes), with the exception of personality disorder, which is an Axis II diagnosis (i.e., considered to be an enduring personality trait).

Thought Disorders

There is neither definitive evidence nor one theory regarding the causes of mental disorders. It is generally believed that a person may inherit a predisposition toward a disorder, which can manifest under stress or because of particular life experiences. There seem to be a disproportionate number of people who have experienced severe abuse, economic, social, and/or political marginalization who have a diagnosis of mental illness (Penney, in press). However, a mental disorder is in no way limited to these groups of individuals.

Schizophrenia Schizophrenia is a complicated disorder that involves both cognitive and emotional dysfunctions, including both negative and positive symptoms (APA, 1994). One psychiatrist explained the complexity of this disorder in the following terms: "How wonderful it would be if two psychiatrists could conceptually agree on what it is" (Pardes, cited in Karno, 1989, p. 1). Schizophrenia is often defined as a group of disorders with one subtype having hallucinations and delusions, and another demonstrating withdrawal, poor personal hygiene, and little spontaneous speech (Altshuler, 1991).

The DSM-IV (APA, 1994) lists five characteristic symptoms of schizophrenia. Four are positive symptoms, or symptoms that are manifested by the individual; the fifth symptom is negative, which includes attributes or characteristics that are not manifested by the individual. The positive symptoms include the following:

- Delusions
- Hallucinations
- Disorganized speech
- Grossly disorganized behavior

Delusions Delusions are distortions or exaggerations in inferential thinking. This misinterpretation of perception or experience can include a variety of themes. The different types of themes include the following:

- *Persecutory:* The individual believes that he or she is being persecuted, perhaps by the Federal Bureau of Investigation or the Internal Revenue Service.
- *Referential:* The individual believes that someone is staring at him or her and reading his or her mind.
- *Somatic:* The individual believes that someone has implanted an electrode in his or her brain.

- *Religious:* The individual believes he or she is an important religious figure, such as the Dalai Lama.
- *Grandiose:* The individual believes he or she can do anything, such as paint a masterpiece or save a nation.

Hallucinations Auditory hallucinations are the most common and characteristic type of symptom of schizophrenia. They include voices that may or may not be recognized as the voice of someone the person knows or that are different from his or her own voice. The voices are usually inside the person's head and may talk to one another or maintain a running commentary on the person's thoughts or behavior. Frequently they are threatening or pejorative. Other hallucinations may be visual, olfactory, gustatory, or tactile.

Disorganized Speech Disorganized speech is exhibited when a person is unable to stay on track. The person's conversations will not make logical sense, or his or her responses may be so obliquely related to the conversation that they may be confusing to the listener. The person's speech can be so disorganized that it is difficult to interpret any meaning. Sometimes it is "word salad" and appears to have no meaning at all.

Grossly Disorganized Behavior Grossly disorganized behavior is when a person experiences severe difficulties in daily living, such as the inability to maintain personal hygiene or to dress appropriately. The person may have difficulty completing tasks or exhibit agitation that appears to have no reason.

Negative Symptoms Included within negative symptoms of schizophrenia is *affective flattening,* which is when a person neither shows nor appears to feel any emotion, regardless of the circumstances. The individual's face may appear immobile and unresponsive to eye contact. The individual also may appear to have few, if any, thoughts, or he or she may speak very little or infrequently. Often the individual does not initiate any goal-directed activities in his or her life.

In the DSM-IV, the APA stated, "Although basic intellectual functions are classically considered to be intact in schizophrenia, some indications of cognitive dysfunction are often present" (1994, p. 277). Accompanying the symptoms of schizophrenia are usually occupational and social dysfunctioning. People with schizophrenia may have difficulty holding a job over a period of time, and they may have difficulties in interpersonal relationships and self-care.

The onset of schizophrenia usually occurs between the late teen years and the mid-30s. The prevalence rate is between .05% and 1% of the U.S. population (National Alliance of the Mentally Ill [NAMI], 1996b). Schizophrenia tends to run in families, and individuals in families with a history of schizophrenia are 10 times more likely to develop the disorder than individuals in the general population.

Possible causes of schizophrenia include heredity and/or viral infections early in life, mild brain damage from complications during birth, or life experiences. Researchers believe that people who develop schizophrenia, similar to individuals who have heart disease, cancer, diabetes, or any chronic illness, may inherit a genetic predisposition to develop the disorder under some conditions. Schizophrenia is not caused by bad parenting or "weak character."

Primary treatment of schizophrenia consists of the use of antipsychotic medications to correct chemical imbalances in the brain. Because schizophrenia may result in difficulties in daily living, rehabilitation services to assist people or to restore them to previous levels of functioning are often helpful. Various therapy modalities also may contribute to better understanding of the illness and how to cope with it.

Studies have shown that after 10 years of treatment, 25% of those with schizophrenia have recovered completely; 25% have considerably improved; 25% have improved modestly; 15% have not improved; and 10% have died, usually by suicide or in an accident (NAMI, 1996d).

Mood Disorders

The primary symptoms of mood disorders are disturbances of mood, "either a depressed mood or a loss of interest or pleasure in nearly all activities" (APA, 1994, p. 320). The category of mood disorders contains, among others, two common diagnoses: 1) major depressive disorder and 2) bipolar disorder.

Major Depressive Disorder   Major depressive disorder is characterized by feelings of worthlessness and guilt; difficulty in thinking or making decisions; and changes in weight or appetite, sleep patterns, or physical activity. Symptoms include recurrent thoughts of death or suicide ideation and plans or attempts to commit suicide. A person who is depressed may exhibit tearfulness, irritability, brooding, obsessive rumination, anxiety, phobias, excessive worries about physical health, and complaints of pain (e.g., headaches, joint and abdominal pains) (APA, 1994). People with depression rarely behave in bizarre ways, almost never experience hallucinations, and only rarely experience delusions. However, about half of the people who commit suicide in the United States have a diagnosis of depression (NAMI, 1996b).

Impairments of social, occupational, or other areas of functioning may accompany depression. People may be unable to continue to work or to go to school. In some severe instances, the person may be unable to either feed or clothe him- or herself or maintain minimal personal hygiene.

Studies indicate that depressive episodes occur twice as frequently in woman as in men (NAMI, 1996b). Adult rates are highest in the 24- to 44-year-old age group, and the average age of onset is in the mid-20s. Symptoms usually develop over several days or weeks. An untreated episode may last 6 months or longer. In the majority of instances, there is a complete remission of symptoms. However, there is a high probability of recurrence once a depression has been experienced.

It is believed that there is no single cause of major depression. Some depressions occur spontaneously and are not associated with any life crisis or physical illness. Others may be brought on by a major loss or change or chronic stress. There appears to be a biological vulnerability to depression that is inherited.

Depression is extremely responsive to treatment. Eighty percent of people with serious depression can improve and return to their normal daily activities (NAMI, 1996b). Medication is used to treat the symptoms of depression in combination with psychological interventions, such as interpersonal therapy or cognitive/behavioral therapy and community support. In cases that do not respond to this type of treatment, electroconvulsive therapy, a highly controversial treatment, is used by some hospitals. If left untreated, severe depression may lead to suicide, which is the eighth leading cause of death in the United States (NAMI, 1996b).

Bipolar Disorder People with bipolar disorder, also called manic depression, experience mood swings that alternate between periods of severe highs (mania) and severe lows (depression). Manic episodes occur immediately after or before a depressive episode in 60%–70% of the instances (APA, 1994). Manic episodes are characterized by inflated self-esteem or grandiosity, decreased need for sleep, feverish activity and productivity, distractibility, and agitation. The person may experience a euphoric or persistently high, elevated mood. When sleep disturbance is severe, the person may go without sleep for days and not feel tired. Many people describe the manic phase of their illness as the most enjoyable time in their lives. However, decisions made during this phase are often reckless and shortsighted.

Because a person with a bipolar disorder alternates between depression and mania, there are usually episodes of alternating depression and mania of characteristic lengths. However, there may be periods of fairly normal activities lasting for months or even years between the episodes. Each person's cycle is unique. Psychotic symptoms may develop as the illness progresses.

Manic depression is believed to be the result of a chemical imbalance in the brain. There appears to be a hereditary predisposition to the disorder. A major loss or change in a person's life in combination with the factors previously discussed may also bring on the illness.

Bipolar disorder is treated similarly to depression. Medication is a critical component of the therapy in most instances. It is also important for the person to recognize the pattern of his or her illness and the cycles of mania and depression and to make life changes that enhance his or her health and sense of well-being. The person may need supportive counseling as well as other forms of therapy and community support. After accurate diagnosis, individuals with manic depression can be successfully treated with medication in 80%–90% of the instances (NAMI, 1996c).

Anxiety Disorders

Anxiety, as it refers to a mental disorder, is an unpleasant and overriding tension that has no apparent identifiable cause. Symptoms can be so severe that people who experience them are almost totally nonfunctional. People with anxiety disorders can be terrified to leave their homes, to use an elevator, or to shop for food. Symptoms include excessive worry, unrealistic fears, "flashbacks," sleep disturbances, shakiness, dizziness, ritualistic behaviors, racing or pounding heart, numbness of hands or feet or other body parts, fatigue, and muscle aches (APA, 1996). Anxiety disorders include panic attacks, phobias, obsessive-compulsive disorders, and posttraumatic stress disorders.

Panic Attack   A person having a panic attack (i.e., feelings of intense fear or discomfort) may experience some of the following feelings:

- Shortness of breath
- Dizziness or faintness
- Elevated heart rate
- Chest pain
- Trembling or shaking
- Sweating
- Choking
- Nausea or abdominal distress
- Fear of dying, losing control, or becoming psychotic

Panic attacks may begin with sudden feelings of fear or impending doom. They usually last minutes rather than hours and may begin unexpectedly, unless the person has identified a particular situation in the past as anxiety provoking (e.g., being in a crowd, being on a bridge, traveling in a bus or a plane). Panic attacks are often associated with agoraphobia (i.e., fear of being in places from which escape is difficult or from which help may be unavailable). People may restrict their activities in order to avoid the fearful situations.

The average age of onset of a panic disorder is between 20 and 30 years of age. Panic attacks may occur several times a week or even daily, and the disorder may persist for years. Women are much more likely to have panic attacks than men. It is not clear what causes any of the anxiety disorders, but it is believed to be a brain dysfunction.

Treatment for a panic disorder is often a combination of medication to block the panic attack and cognitive therapy to help the person manage the panic-provoking situations. Psychotherapy, healthy living habits, and peer support are also helpful. Treatment can be successful: 70%–90% of those treated show significant improvement (NAMI, 1996a).

Phobia Phobia is an anxiety disorder that is characterized by feelings of terror, dread, or panic when a person is confronted with a feared object, situation, or activity (APA, 1996). They may have such an overwhelming need to avoid the source of fear that it interferes with their work, family, and social life. The following are common phobias:

- Social phobia
- Simple phobia
- Agoraphobia

Social Phobia Social phobia is the fear of being humiliated or embarrassed in front of people. People with social phobias may avoid situations in which they can be watched by others, such as public speaking or eating in public. Although social phobias may sometimes be mistaken for shyness, they are much more extreme. Social phobias often begin in late childhood or during early adolescence. They may be related to feelings of inferiority or low self-esteem. As of 1998, there is no proven drug intervention to use with social phobias, but certain medications may be given to help reduce symptoms of anxiety. *Desensitization,* a form of cognitive behavioral therapy that exposes people to what frightens them, is one recommended intervention (National Mental Health Association, 1997).

Simple Phobia Simple phobia is the fear of specific objects or situations that cause terror. Examples are fear of snakes, flying, bridges, heights, or enclosed places. People who have simple phobia know that their fear is irrational, but the object or situation still causes extreme anxiety. Approximately 12% of all Americans have phobias. They are the most common psychiatric illnesses in women and the second most common in men older than 25 years of age (National Mental Health Association, 1997). Simple phobias seem to run in families. Antidepressants have proven effective in treatment.

Agoraphobia Agoraphobia is the fear of being in a public place or in situations from which it might be difficult or embarrassing to escape, such as an elevator or a room full of people. Agoraphobia often occurs in combination with panic attacks (National Mental Health Association, 1997). Agoraphobia is extremely disabling because people can become housebound as a result of it. People become fearful of leaving their homes because they may have a panic attack. The same interventions that are commonly used for treating social phobias are also used in assisting individuals with agoraphobia.

Obsessive-Compulsive Disorder   Obsessive-compulsive disorder is characterized by persistent, unwelcome thoughts and rituals that one cannot control. The intrusive thoughts are called *obsessions;* the rituals, which are performed to try to prevent or dispel those obsessions, are called *compulsions.* Those who have this disorder may have an excessive need to be orderly, perfect, and in control. They often are "Type A" personalities working and being productive at the expense of any relaxation or friendship. They may be so concerned with "doing it right" that they are unable to complete tasks or to accept help from others. People with obsessive-compulsive disorder often exhibit an extreme rigidity related to morality, ethics, and values and/or a miserly attitude toward money. These individuals also may hoard and retain things to the extent that it becomes extremely dysfunctional.

The need for control in people with an obsessive-compulsive disorder may manifest itself through either extreme adherence to rules or extreme attendance to details or procedures. The person may become deeply upset if things change and appear to be out of his or her control. He or she is often extremely stubborn and rigid and may be unaware of or does not respond to the effect that he or she has on others. The person's relationships may have a distant and formal quality. In addition, he or she may be uncomfortable with expressed feelings and unable to respond spontaneously and happily to joyful events.

According to the DSM-IV (APA, 1994), obsessive-compulsive disorder appears twice as often in men as in women and occurs in approximately 1% of the U.S. population. It is believed to run in families. Medication and behavior therapy may be used to effectively treat the disorder. Behavior therapy attempts to change a person's behavior by deliberately exposing them to the feared object or idea—either directly or through their imaginations—and then teaches them to respond in a more effective way than the compulsive behavior pattern.

Posttraumatic Stress Disorder   Posttraumatic stress disorder may occur when a person experiences, witnesses, or hears about an extremely stressful or traumatic event usually involving death, threatened death, serious injury, or threat to one's own or another person's physical integrity. Examples might include violent physical attack, torture, sexual assault, being taken as a hostage or prisoner of war, natural or man-made disasters, serious automobile accidents, or being diagnosed with a life-threatening illness.

Symptoms of posttraumatic stress disorder usually begin 3 months or more after the trauma. They include reexperiencing the trauma through recollection, dreams, and dissociative flashback episodes. Individuals with posttraumatic stress disorder may experience amnesia with regard to aspects of the trauma and persistently avoid anything related to the trauma, including places, people, thoughts, feelings, or conversations. (They may limit their activities to do so.) Correspondingly, they may have feelings of detachment, restriction of feelings (termed *psychic numbing*), and a sense of an early death. They may have difficulty sleeping, concentrating, or completing tasks. Other symptoms include hypervigilance, irritability with bursts of anger, and an exaggerated startle response.

Posttraumatic stress disorder can occur at any age, including childhood. Prevalence within the U.S. population has been measured at 1%–14% (APA, 1994). Combat veterans, victims of severe natural disasters or criminal violence, or other individuals at risk have a prevalence rate ranging from 3% to 58% (APA, 1994).

Treatment for posttraumatic stress disorder consists of antidepressants; anxiety-reducing medications; and cognitive-behavioral therapy, which teaches the person new ways to think about events and circumstances in his or her life. Reactions can thus be modified in situations that bring on the symptoms of stress.

Dissociative Disorders

The essential feature of a dissociative disorder is a disruption in a person's usually integrated functions of consciousness, memory, identity, and perception of the environment. The disturbance may be sudden, gradual, transient, or chronic.

Dissociative identity disorder, formerly known as *multiple personality disorder,* is characterized by the presence of two or more distinct identities or personalities in a person that repeatedly take over behavior. Each identity may have a distinct personal history, characteristics, knowledge, age, gender, and name that usually cannot be recalled when another personality is in control. Usually there is a primary identity, but it may be passive and depressed.

Transition among identities may be triggered by stress and occur within seconds. The number of identities reported range greatly, but half of the instances have 10 or fewer. Individuals with dissociative personality disorder have frequently experienced severe physical and sexual abuse, particularly during childhood. Adult females are diagnosed three to nine times more frequently than adult males (APA,

1994). In children, the ratio of male to female is more even. The disorder has a fluctuating clinical course that tends to be chronic and recurrent. There appears to be a rise in the number of people with this diagnosis for reasons that are unclear. Treatment for dissociative identity disorder includes the use of medication and psychotherapy.

Personality Disorders

Personality traits are those enduring patterns of thinking, feeling, and behaving that make us who we are. Personality disorders occur when these personality traits become inflexible and maladaptive, causing distress and functional impairment.

Borderline Personality Disorder   The APA defined *borderline personality disorder* as a "pervasive pattern of instability of interpersonal relationships, self-image, and affects, and marked impulsivity that begins by early childhood and is present in a variety of contexts" (1994, p. 650). People with this disorder may have intense fears of abandonment and may experience extreme anger when faced with realistic separation or limit setting on the part of people with whom they have relationships.

Their relationships are frequently intense and unstable, and they form intimate bonds extremely quickly. However, their feelings can change abruptly and dramatically if they feel that the other person does not care or give enough to them. Their self-image, goals, and values also may change abruptly, and they may have difficulty in unstructured work or school situations. Their self-images might be based on being bad or evil. Some individuals believe that they do not exist at all or have chronic feelings of emptiness.

Characteristics of people with borderline personality disorder include irresponsible behaviors in situations such as driving, recklessly spending money, using drugs, or having unsafe sex. Repeated suicide gestures or attempts and frequent self-mutilations can also occur. They can experience extreme mood swings and be easily bored. If they perceive a lover or caregiver to be neglectful, they may react with an intense verbal outburst and be extremely sarcastic and bitter.

The most common course of this disorder is a pattern of chronic instability in early adulthood, with greater stability reached during the individual's 30s and 40s. Premature death by suicide occurs in 8%–10% of these individuals. Seventy-five percent of the instances identified are women. It is five times more common in biological relatives than in the general population. The prevalence rate is estimated to be about

2% (APA, 1994). (See Chapter 6 for further discussion.) Treatments for borderline personality disorder include medication and cognitive behavioral therapy with an emphasis on restructuring the individual's thought processes.

DUAL DIAGNOSIS: MENTAL DISORDERS AND SUBSTANCE ABUSE

It is estimated that between one third and one half of all psychiatric patients also abuse drugs or alcohol (Safer, 1987). Both types of diagnosis—mental disorders and substance abuse—can be chronic disorders with independent courses that exacerbate one another. Drug effects, however, can mimic psychiatric symptoms, so diagnostic confusion is common until an extended period of abstinence can be achieved. Poor treatment compliance, coupled with frequent brief hospitalizations until the disorder is diagnosed and treated, is often the norm.

Psychiatric medications must be carefully prescribed and monitored for people with a dual diagnosis because of increased risks of abuse and overdose. Many psychiatrists are reluctant to prescribe medications until a person is drug or alcohol free and in a treatment environment. Some psychotropic medications can be cross-addicting. Although both mental illness and substance abuse can cause multiple disabilities, treatment systems are separate and not well-integrated. Mental health treatment and drug and alcohol treatment have differing philosophies, staff training, policies, and procedures (Carey, 1989).

Many people with a mental illness begin or continue to use alcohol or drugs to lessen the symptoms of a mental illness, either before or after it has been diagnosed (APA, 1995). Treatment of alcohol or drug abuse with people with mental illness consists of detoxification followed by medication and therapy programs. After abstinence and treatment, many people attend self-help groups such as Alcoholics Anonymous and Narcotics Anonymous. These groups are located in almost all towns and cities, have frequent meetings, and provide ongoing support.

WARNING SIGNS OF MENTAL ILLNESS

The onset of a mental illness often happens over time. The person affected or his or her friends and family may not be aware of what is happening or what dramatic changes in behavior may mean. Many have had no experience with people with mental illness and do not recognize some of the warning signs. Early diagnosis of mental illness is important to prevent deterioration of behavior and loss of aspirations. Early intervention, with treatment and medication, can lessen the need for rehabilitation services later.

The National Mental Health Association (1997) listed the following common warning signs of mental illness:

- Confused thinking
- Prolonged depression (i.e., sadness or irritability)
- Feelings of extreme highs or lows
- Excessive fears, worries, and anxieties
- Social withdrawal
- Dramatic changes in eating or sleeping habits
- Strong feelings of anger
- Delusions or hallucinations
- Growing inability to cope with daily problems and activities
- Suicidal thoughts
- Denial of obvious problems
- Numerous unexplained physical ailments
- Substance abuse
- Changes in eating or sleeping habits
- Changes in school or work performance

STIGMA ASSOCIATED WITH MENTAL ILLNESS

Mental illness is not seen as an illness or disorder in the same way that other chronic illnesses are viewed. People with mental illness are often the victims of stigma. *Merriam-Webster's Collegiate Dictionary* defined *stigma* as "a mark of shame or discredit" (1996, p. 1155). The label of mental illness carries with it shame and discredit: shame on the part of the person with the diagnosis and discredit on the part of the person interacting with the person with the diagnosis. Coleman (cited in Reidy, 1994) identified three major effects of stigma: 1) social rejection or isolation, 2) lowered expectations, and 3) internalized stigma.

Social Rejection or Isolation

The mental health system in the past has separated and isolated people through hospitalizations, group homes, and day treatment centers. Although some progress has been made, few individuals receive treatment that is designed to integrate them back into more meaningful roles and activities within their communities (Reidy, 1994). Many individuals are also separated when they are not fully accepted into social situations or into equal roles when they are at work or at school.

Lowered Expectations

Lowered expectations come from not only the mental health system but also the people who are involved in the system themselves. Because people with mental illness are often stereotyped, they are discouraged from having high expectations. The "mentally ill" label carries with it a sentence of "different" and "less than." This reinforces low self-esteem, which in turn makes it difficult to create or take advantage of many opportunities. It also leads to internalized stigma, which is the essence of low self-esteem (Reidy, 1994).

Internalized Stigma

In a qualitative survey (Reidy, 1994) conducted in Massachusetts, individuals identified internalized stigma (i.e., incorporating the society's values into one's own values) as the most devastating effect of stigma. Fisher said the following in regard to the stigma of his mental illness diagnosis:

> It took me a long time to regain my self-esteem. I almost did have to become a psychiatrist to regain my self-esteem—to prove to myself, to prove to the world, to overcome the labels. Once they've done that diagnosis, you just can't get rid of it, from their records, and your heart. (cited in Reidy, 1994, p. 7)

Another effect of internalized stigma is depression. A respondent in Reidy's study said, "I've been psychologized so much, it's ridiculous! I'm helpless, hopeless, lost, frustrated, discouraged, confused—not depressed" (1994, p. 8). Other respondents felt they carried a label that would be with them for the rest of their lives, and it colored everything that they did or thought about themselves.

Poverty is one of the most debilitating effects of stigma. People who are unable to work as a result of their illness are eligible for Social Security Disability Insurance (SSDI). However, the amount of money from SSDI makes it possible to live only in the cheapest, most undesirable, and often unsafe housing. There is seldom money to support an adequate diet. Any emergency can be devastating. The Social Security Administration can arbitrarily change or reduce benefits, sometimes for unpredictable reasons. The uncertainty and anxiety of living on the edge contributes to the other manifestations of stigma and results in making recovering from a mental illness even more difficult.

PERCEIVED DANGERS OF
PEOPLE WITH MENTAL ILLNESS

There continues to be controversy about the perceived dangers of people with mental illness. In the late 1980s and early 1990s, a number of research articles appeared in an effort to answer questions surrounding the issue (Burke, 1990; Dvoskin, 1990; Shah, 1990; Steadman, 1983; Steadman & Felson, 1984; Teplin, 1985). Each article presented a different perspective; outcomes depended on the populations surveyed, how the questions were asked, and when and where the study was conducted. For example, self-report data were used to compare the relative incidences of aggression with violence among ex–mental patients, ex-offenders, and the general population (Steadman & Felson, 1984). The evidence suggested that ex-offenders engaged in violence with greater frequency than ex–mental patients and the general population and have a greater tendency to physically attack and injure their antagonists when involved in violent disputes.

In another study that examined the issue of the perceived dangers of individuals with mental illness, Teplin (1985) presented observational data from 1,072 police–citizen encounters in an urban area. The data showed that individuals exhibiting signs of serious mental illness were not suspected of serious crimes at a rate disproportionate to their numbers in the general population. The patterns of crime for individuals with mental illness compared with that of individuals without mental illness were substantially similar. "These data," stated Teplin, "help dispel the myth that the mentally ill constitute a dangerous group prone to violent crime" (1985, p. 597).

Mental health professionals are often asked to predict how dangerous someone will be. A comprehensive study by Steadman (1983) examined the accuracy of psychiatric predictions of perceived danger. He concluded that mental health professionals were no more accurate at predicting dangerousness than the general public.

Dvoskin stated that "it is clear that mental illness by itself does not necessarily increase the probability of violent behavior. But for some people, in some circumstances, it may" (1990, p. 6). He went on to say that "judgments about groups of people can only lead to stigma and discrimination, while judgments about individuals, if based on reason and information, can lead to better treatment outcomes and increased safety for the individuals and their communities" (p. 6). He also noted that some people with mental illness behave violently only when they are drunk, while others behave violently only when they are not taking their medication.

In somewhat the same vein, Burke (1990) analyzed a study with 10,000 individuals who had participated in a National Institutes of Health study. The outcomes indicated that survey respondents with anxiety disorders had about the same rate of violence or assaultive behavior (approximately 2.4%) in the year prior to the interview as those respondents who had no mental disorder. Individuals with a diagnosis of depression or bipolar disorder reported approximately the same rate of violence (3.4%). A diagnosis of schizophrenia presented a greater risk, and the risk was even higher when an individual with this diagnosis abused drugs or alcohol. However, Burke stated, "For members of the general public, it appears that the greatest community exposure to violence may come from alcoholic individuals, not from those persons with serious disorders like schizophrenia" (1990, p. 18).

A similar conclusion was reached by Shah who stated, "Among persons suffering from serious mental disorders (e.g., schizophrenia, mood disorders), those with co-occurring substance abuse, and especially those with prior histories of assaultive and violent behaviors, will typically present increased risks of violence" (1990, p. 20). Shah also noted that many people with a major mental illness diagnosis (i.e., anxiety and depressive disorders) will generally have a lower incidence of criminal and violent behavior toward others.

Some individuals with mental illness are jailed or imprisoned when, in fact, they are in need of psychiatric care (Sullivan & Spritzer, 1997). With restrictive admissions policies at public inpatient facilities, rates of arrest and incarceration of people with mental illness have been increasing. Seventy-five percent of people with mental illness who were jailed ($N = 177$)—most for more than 5 days—in a rural state were incarcerated at some time in their lives without charges while waiting for a hospital bed at a facility (Sullivan & Spritzer, 1997). Because there was no room for them at a psychiatric hospital or treatment center, they were held in jail while awaiting treatment.

SUMMARY

Mental illness is a complex disorder, and individuals—even if they have a similar diagnosis—can experience the same disorder differently. As a result, treatment and services need to be individualized. Although mental illness has been believed to be a chronic, lifelong illness, research has demonstrated that in most cases it is not. Symptoms can abate, and most people with a mental illness can resume their normal lives. Stigma, however, continues to be a problem, and, more precisely, the fear that people with a mental disorder may be dangerous continues to be a threat. It is as important that attitudes and prejudices about mental illness change through greater understanding and knowledge as it is for new medications and treatments to be developed.

REFERENCES

Altshuler, L. (1991). Neuroanatomy in schizophrenia and affective disorder. *The Journal of the California Alliance for the Mentally Ill*, 2(4), 27–30.

American Psychiatric Association. (1994). *Diagnostic and statistical manual of mental disorders* (4th ed.). Washington, DC: Author.

American Psychiatric Association. (1995). *Let's talk facts about: Mental illness: An overview*. Washington, DC: Author.

American Psychiatric Association. (1996). *Let's talk facts about: Anxiety disorders*. Washington, DC: Author.

Bond, G.R., Drake, R.E., Mueser, K.T., & Becker, D.R. (1997). An update on supported employment for people with severe mental illness. *Psychiatric Services*, 48(3), 335–346.

Burke, J.D. (1990). Two decades of research. *The Journal of the Alliance for the Mentally Ill*, 2(1), 18.

Carey, K.B. (1989). Emerging treatment guidelines for mentally ill chemical abusers. *Hospital and Community Psychiatry*, 40(4), 341–349.

Drake, R.E., Becker R.B., Biesanz, B.A., Torrey, W.C., McHugo, G.J., & Wyzik, P.F. (1994). Rehabilitative day treatment vs. supported employment: I. Vocational outcomes. *Community Mental Health Journal*. 30(5), 519–531.

Dvoskin, J. (1990). What are the odds of predicting violent behavior? *The Journal of the California Alliance for the Mentally Ill*, 2(1), 6–7.

Erikson, E.H. (1963). *Childhood and society* (Rev. ed.). New York: W.W. Norton.

Harding, C.M. (1988). The outcome of schizophrenia. *The Harvard Medical School Mental Health Letter*, 4(11), 3–5.

Havighurst, R.J. (1972). *Developmental tasks and education* (3rd ed.). New York: Longman.

Jaffe, M. (1993). Posters, posters. *The Journal of the California Alliance for the Mentally Ill*, 4(1), 61–62.

Karno, M. (1989, Summer). Inside this issue. *The Journal of the California Alliance for the Mentally Ill*, 1(1), 1–3.

Merriam-Webster's Collegiate Dictionary (10th ed.). (1996). Springfield, MA: Merriam-Webster.

Monahan, J., & Arnold, J. (1996). Violence by people with mental illness: A consensus statement by advocates and researchers. *Psychiatric Rehabilitation Journal*, 19(4), 67–70.

National Alliance for the Mentally Ill. (1996a). Panic disorder. *NAMI Medical Information Series*. Arlington, VA: Author.

National Alliance for the Mentally Ill. (1996b). *Understanding major depression: What you need to know about this medical illness*. Arlington, VA: Author.

National Alliance for the Mentally Ill. (1996c). *Understanding manic depression: What you need to know about this medical illness*. Arlington, VA: Author.

National Alliance for the Mentally Ill. (1996d). *Understanding schizophrenia: What you need to know about this medical illness*. Arlington, VA: Author.

National Mental Health Association. (1997). *Anxiety disorders: What you need to know*. Alexandria, VA: Author.

Neugeboren, J. (1997). *Imagining Robert, my brother, madness and survival: A memoir.* New York: William Morrow & Co.

Parton, D. (1993). Implementation of a systems approach to supported education at four California Community College model service sites. *Psychosocial Rehabilitation Journal, 17*(1), 171–188.

Penney, D. (in press). Redefining medical necessity: Toward development of a recovery-oriented mental health benefit. In C. Stoud (Ed.), *The complete guide to managed behavioral healthcare.* New York: John Wiley & Sons.

Peschel, E., & Peschel, R. (1991, Summer). Neurobiological disorders. *The Journal of the California Alliance for the Mentally Ill, 2*(4), 4.

Reidy, D. (1994). Recovering from treatment: The mental health system as agent of stigma. *Resources, 6*(3) 3–10.

Safer, D.J. (1987). Substance abuse by young adult chronic patients. *Hospital and Community Psychiatry, 38,* 511–514.

Shah, S. (1990). Violence and the mentally ill. *The Journal of the California Alliance for the Mentally Ill, 2*(1), 20–21.

Steadman, H. (1983). Predicting dangerousness among the mentally ill: Art, magic and science. *International Journal of Law and Psychiatry, 6,* 381–390.

Steadman, H., & Felson, R.B. (1984). Self-reports of violence: Ex-mental patients, ex-offenders and the general public. *Criminology, 22,* 321–342.

Sullivan, F., & Spritzer, K. (1997). The criminalization of persons with serious mental illness living in rural areas. *Journal of Rural Health, 13*(1), 6–13.

Teplin, L. (1985). The criminality of the mentally ill: A dangerous misconception. *American Journal of Psychiatry, 142,* 593–599.

Unger, K. (1997). *Case studies of people with mental illness who have returned to college.* Unpublished manuscript. Tucson: University of Arizona, Community Rehabilitation Division.

Wirshing, W. (1991). Searching the brain: Trying to see neurobiological disorders. *The Journal of the California Alliance for the Mentally Ill, 2*(4), 2–3.

Treatment
and Interventions
for Mental Illness

I had been in the mental health system on and off for 12 years . . . .
I had been hospitalized several times and each time I acquired a
new diagnosis. The first diagnosis was schizophrenia. From there
I was labeled schizoid, schizoaffective, schizotypal, bipolar I and
bipolar II, dysthymic, major depression, and, of course, personal-
ity disorder. I had been labeled at least eight of the twelve possi-
bilities, both separately and in combination. Each new diagnosis
required a new regimen of medications to control the symptoms.
(Risser, 1992, p. 38)

For paid professionals, then, to act as if Robert were merely a ves-
sel of flesh in which (bad) chemicals somehow rose up once upon a
time and made him ill, and in which other (good) chemicals must
now be poured in order to either cure him or keep him quiet—this
is not merely the dead end of a scientific materialism not so differ-
ent from (ineffective) witchcraft, but it deprives Robert, to put it
most simply, of what he still possesses in abundance: his human-
ity. (Neugeboren, 1997, p. 136)

When I started down the road of psychiatric medication, I was
quiet and embarrassed. I was afraid of condemnation. I felt shame

when I went to the pharmacy and filled my prescriptions. How-
ever, the pain was so great that I was willing to try anything. I
could not go on living as I had been. The bouts of penetrating de-
spair were bringing me to my knees and suicide was a looming re-
ality. (Collier, 1993, p. 16)

In addition to improved understanding of how the brain functions, there have been corresponding improvements in medications and interventions for treating mental illness. This chapter reviews some of the psychotropic medications that are most frequently used in the care of mental illness; describes treatment and intervention modalities; and details the kinds of professionals who provide these types of treatments, interventions, and services. In addition, mental health and other types of service agencies (e.g., psychosocial, employment, housing, financial) and programs are also explained.

PSYCHOTROPIC MEDICATIONS

Psychotropic medications, as with most other medications, can have severe side effects. Just as heart disease medication can cause low blood pressure or antibiotics can cause nausea, psychotropic medications can interfere, sometimes severely, with bodily or daily functioning. Side effects vary with each person and with the dosage of medication or medications necessary. Sometimes several medications are prescribed, one as the medication to address the major problem and the others to alleviate or mitigate the primary medication's side effects. A holistic approach to health and mental health care, with medication as one intervention, is the most effective means to recovery.

Side Effects of Psychotropic Medications

The American Psychiatric Association (APA) (1993) listed the following side effects of psychotropic medications, which are unique to this type of medication:

Akathisia: A feeling of restlessness and inability to sit still. This side effect is difficult to treat and affects up to 75% of those treated with neuroleptic medication.
Dystonia: Painful, tightening spasms of the muscles, particularly those of the face and neck. This complication affects 1%–8% of those

who take neuroleptic medications and is treatable with other medications.

Parkinsonism: A group of symptoms that resembles those brought on by Parkinson's disease, including loss of facial expression, slowed movements, rigidity in arms and legs, drooling, and/or shuffling gait. It affects up to 33% of those taking neuroleptic medications and is treatable with other medications.

Tardive dyskinesia: Involuntary muscular movements that can affect any muscle group but most often affect facial muscles. Characteristic involuntary movements include tongue rolling, chewing movements, pilling with fingers, or grimacing and/or frowning. The condition manifests in 20%–25% of the people taking antipsychotic medications. It is one of the most serious side effects of antipsychotic medications, and there is no known cure. If tardive dyskinesia begins to develop, medications are usually discontinued.

People with psychiatric disorders are sometimes described as *noncompliant* if they do not take their medications. Many people choose not to take their medications because of the discomfort or inconvenience of the side effects. However, the medications are extremely useful for most people in controlling the symptoms of a mental illness; they generally make it possible to take advantage of therapy, self-help groups, and supportive services, as well as to return to school or work. Medications, however, should be taken only after a person has received a complete medical and physical exam and is properly monitored for both the medicine's benefits and side effects (APA, 1993).

There has been a dramatic growth in successful drug research involving psychotropic medications since the mid-1980s. Scientists are working on drugs that more specifically target areas and functions of the brain. Neuroimaging advances have made it possible to both isolate areas of the brain that are affected by mental illness and target the medications to various brain receptors. The newer medications are often more effective and have fewer side effects than the older medications.

Antipsychotic medications are the most common medications used to counteract psychotic and catatonic symptoms and stop delusions and hallucinations. However, the side effects can be uncomfortable and debilitating. (For further information on all medications and their side effects, consult the *Physician's Desk Reference*, 1998).

Psychotropic Drugs

Chlorpromazine (Thorazine), *haloperidol* (Haldol), *trifluoperazine* (Stelazine), and *fluphenazine* (Prolixin) are conventional medications that affect the dopamine levels of the brain. These medications are powerful antipsychotics that control symptoms of mental illness for many people. However, the side effects may include dry mouth, constipation, urinary retention, blurred vision, tachycardia (i.e., rapid heartbeat), confusion, memory disruption, sedation, weight gain, and muscle rigidity. Tardive dyskinesia is also a side effect that sometimes occurs after the long-term use of these drugs.

Clozapine (Clozaril) is a new antipsychotic medication that came on the market in 1990. It is most effective for the positive symptoms of schizophrenia (e.g., hallucinations, delusions). Although Clozaril has fewer side effects than some of the older medications, it may cause sedation, hypersalivation, transient fever, weight gain, tachycardia, constipation, or seizures. In addition, those who use the medication need weekly blood tests to check white blood cell count levels.

Risperidone (Risperdal) is able to manage both the positive as well as some of the negative symptoms of schizophrenia. However, Risperdal seems to block the action of serotonin and dopamine, neurotransmitter chemicals in the brain. Side effects are relatively minor in most people. It is considered the first drug of choice for a person newly diagnosed with schizophrenia. Side effects may include low blood pressure, dizziness, sleepiness, weight gain, sexual dysfunction, and fatigue.

Olanzapine (Zyprexa) came on the market at the end of 1996. It is similar in its effect to clozapine, but its side effects are different. It may have a greater risk of causing extrapyramidal side effects (e.g., slowing of voluntary movements, expressionless face, rigidity and tremor of arms and head, abnormal toxicity of muscle tissues, restlessness). However, Zyprexa does not cause seizures or agranulocyosis (i.e., a deficiency of a type of white blood cell that can be fatal) and does not require weekly blood testing.

Mood Stabilizing and Antidepressant Drugs

Lithium carbonate has been the most common medication used to reduce both mania and depression. It does not produce sedation or other effects on awareness or mental functioning. Lithium carbonate is relatively safe and effective and can be taken for long periods of time, although it may cause kidney damage or depress thyroid function. Other side effects may include acne, gastrointestinal symptoms, hand tremors, thirst, frequent urination, or weight gain. Blood levels need to be checked frequently to watch for excessive retention of lithium.

There are many new medications to treat depression that have come on the market since 1987 (St. Dennis, 1996). The following are three examples:

Nefazodone **(Serzone):**   Serzone was approved in 1994 and found to be safe and effective during prolonged treatment of depression. Serzone improves depression-related anxiety and relieves depression-related insomnia. It has been found to decrease the amount of wake time and fragmented sleep found in many individuals with depression. Side effects include asthenia (i.e., lack of physical strength), dry mouth, nausea, constipation, drowsiness, dizziness, lightheadedness, confusion, and blurred or abnormal vision. Serzone does not cause weight gain or loss, elevated blood pressure, or sexual dysfunction.

Venlafaxine **(Effexor):**   Effexor was approved in 1993; it is the drug of choice for individuals who have recently been diagnosed with depression. It also can be useful for individuals who have had longstanding depressive illness and have not responded adequately to previous treatments. Side effects include sleepiness, dry mouth, dizziness, constipation, nervousness, sweating, weakness, sexual dysfunction, and loss of appetite.

Fluoxetine **(Prozac):**   Prozac is a new antidepressant drug that has become one of the most widely prescribed medications on the market. It is very effective in relieving symptoms of depression with fewer, milder side effects than other antidepressants. It does not cause dry mouth or weight gain; however, it may cause slight weight loss. The side effects that occur, primarily anxiety, insomnia, drowsiness, headache, diarrhea, and rash, generally subside in a few weeks. It also may inhibit orgasm or cause cravings for alcohol. It is effective in treating depressive disorders, obsessive-compulsive disorders, bulimia nervosa, and panic/agoraphobia disorders.

Medications for Mania

Divalproex sodium (Depakote) was approved in 1995 for the treatment of manic depression (i.e., bipolar disorder) and is the first new medication for treating manic depressive disorder since 1970. Depakote had been used since the mid-1980s as a treatment for epilepsy. Common side effects include nausea, vomiting, weight gain, sedation, and tremor. Liver problems may develop, particularly in the first 6 months of use. *Lithium* (Eskalith or Lithobid) is also used for the treatment of bipolar disorder.

Medications for Anxiety Disorders

Buspirone (Buspar) is a new antianxiety medication that is nonsedating and is not addictive. It does not produce significant functional impairment. The common side effects include dizziness, nausea, headache, nervousness, lightheadedness, and excitement. Prozac is also used as a treatment for anxiety disorders.

Alprazolam (Xanax) is used for the management of anxiety disorders, particularly panic disorders. Side effects, if they do occur, are generally observed at the beginning of therapy and usually disappear after continued medication. The most frequent side effects are drowsiness or lightheadedness.

Paroxetine hydrochloride (Paxil) is an antidepressant that is used for the management of depression, obsessive-compulsive disorders, and panic disorders. The side effects include asthenia, sweating, nausea, decreased appetite, dizziness, nervousness, constipation, insomnia, abnormal ejaculation, and genital disorders.

TREATMENT FOR MENTAL DISORDERS

The deinstitutionalization movement of the early 1970s moved people from the hospital to the community with the belief that individuals with mental illness should receive treatment in their communities. To assist the communities to improve opportunities and services, the National Institutes of Mental Health initiated the Community Support Program (CSP) (Stroul, 1988). The CSP articulated the philosophy that individuals with mental illness are seen first and foremost as people with basic human needs and aspirations and as citizens with all the rights, privileges, opportunities, and responsibilities accorded citizens without mental illness. The CSP advocated for an integrated network of services that was based on the principles that people with a mental illness should have a right to services that were

- Consumer centered and empowering
- Racially and culturally appropriate
- Flexible and focused on their strengths
- Normalized and incorporated the person's natural support systems
- Sensitive to special needs
- Coordinated
- Accountable to the person and his or her family

The CSP provided core values and a framework for agencies to develop a range of options that included housing, employment, education, treatment, health care, financial assistance, rehabilitation services, and peer support. Although not all mental health agencies fully met this challenge, the framework of core values provided a yardstick by which to evaluate programs and an ideal to which to aspire. It is against this backdrop that the following services and service providers are described.

Treatment Modalities

Since the 1970s, treatment modalities have been developed based on learning theory or behaviorism. It is generally understood that if a person's behavior and how he or she thinks about or labels experiences or feelings can be changed, then the person will experience a change in how he or she feels and acts. It also is clear that people can unlearn old patterns of feelings and behavior and learn new, more satisfying and productive patterns.

These beliefs reflect a change in philosophy from the psychodynamic theory, which was historically used in "talk therapies." In these earlier interventions, it was believed that problems resulted from impulses that were largely beyond a person's understanding and were the result of the relationship with his or her parents and other significant individuals. The goal of the therapy was to help people understand the underlying dynamics of their behavior and to make changes based on this increased insight and understanding. Therapies since the 1970s tend to be of shorter duration and more goal oriented and are designed specifically to change behavior.

The names of the newer therapies overlap but are commonly called *cognitive behavior therapy, cognitive therapy*, and *interpersonal therapy*. Although all of these therapies have a common philosophical base, there are some variations in how and why they are utilized.

Cognitive behavior therapy works to change behavior by changing negative styles of thinking and unproductive behavior patterns that contribute to a particular illness. New skills and new ways of thinking are taught to help people react differently to situations that trigger symptoms. Some *cognitive therapies* are effective in helping people to manage frightening situations that may trigger anxiety or panic attacks. They use hierarchical desensitization, gradually exposing the individual to the difficult situation and providing the individual with support as he or she goes through the experience. *Interpersonal therapy* may focus on more effectively dealing with other people to change relationships that exacerbate an illness.

Psychosocial or psychiatric rehabilitation is an intervention that is based on the philosophy that if people learn new skills and are given support, then they can function more independently in the community. For example, if an individual wants a job, an assessment will be conducted to determine the skills needed and the kinds of supports and/

or accommodations needed to be successful at a jobsite. The interventions are skills teaching and providing resources along with personal support.

Standard health practices such as exercise, a healthy diet, adequate sleep and rest, stress management, and moderate use of alcohol and caffeine are also very important in the treatment of a mental illness. Adequate health and dental care are also necessary.

Treatment Professionals

There are many kinds of mental health providers who work with people with mental illness. Although their disciplines may be different, the services they provide can overlap. Some of the major categories of providers include the following:

Psychiatrists: Medical doctors, who in addition to their physical medicine training, have a specialization in psychiatry. Psychiatrists are the only mental health professionals who can prescribe medications.

Clinical psychologists: Individuals who are trained in different therapy modalities and are able to administer psychological tests.

Social workers: Individuals who are trained in counseling, advocacy, and community and family integration. They also may provide service coordinator services. They often take a broad perspective and look at the person in relation to his or her environment.

Case managers: Individuals who coordinate and integrate all of the services that a person may need, including treatment, housing, vocational and educational services, and advocacy. (Some of the service providers previously mentioned also provide case management services.)

Mental health counselors: Individuals who provide counseling services that enhance daily living. They also may provide case management services.

Rehabilitation and/or vocational counselors: Individuals who assist people by helping them return to work or school or to live more independently. They also may act as advocates or as case managers.

Peer support counselors: Individuals with mental illness who help other consumers of the mental health system. In some communities, networks of peer support counselors are being developed, whereas in other mental health agencies, peer counselors are hired to provide support and advocacy to agency consumers. It is believed that people who have utilized the mental health system and have been diagnosed with a mental illness can be very helpful to others with similar experiences.

Family counselors: Individuals who assist families to adjust to the changes in the individual with a mental illness and to adjust to their own feelings for and expectations of this individual. The families of the people with a mental illness often need support and help in coping with the family member who has been diagnosed with the illness.

Treatment Resources

There are services available in the community to assist people with mental illness to function as independently as possible. Although most people who have a disability resulting from a psychiatric condition may receive these services, because of lack of funding for most programs, adequate services frequently are not available. How well people are served depends on the resources and priorities of the individual communities.

Financial Support   If a person has been diagnosed with a mental illness and is unable to work, he or she may be entitled to disability payments from Supplemental Security Income (SSI), Social Security Disability Insurance (SSDI), or General Public Assistance (GPA) through Social Security Administration field offices, which are located in most communities. SSI is a federal and state program that provides income to those who are "aged, blind, or disabled." Eligibility is based on need. SSDI is insurance for workers with a disability but who have paid into the Social Security system through payroll deductions. GPA is available in some locations to those with a disability and who are either ineligible or waiting for other assistance (see Chapter 8 for more information).

Medicaid is a state and federal health insurance program designed for those with low incomes. Eligibility varies from state to state. Many people who receive these types of assistance may also be eligible for food stamps.

Treatment Services   Psychiatric hospitals provide treatment services to people when they are in the acute or psychotic stages of an illness. Treatment usually involves medication to alleviate or minimize the symptoms, some form of therapy and/or rehabilitation, and discharge planning. Most hospital stays are limited, and the emphasis is on stabilizing the person and returning him or her to the community and the services available there.

Crisis intervention services provide emergency help to people in psychiatric crisis. Depending on the severity of the crisis, services may include telephone support; home visits; crisis residence; transportation to and from the hospital; and coordination with hospital staff on admission, release, and treatment. Crisis services are available at most hospitals and through some telephone hot lines.

Community mental health centers are local facilities offering outpatient treatment and emergency services. They often provide a variety of services, including case management, educational and vocational services, advocacy, and self-help groups.

Clubhouse programs are organizations in which people with mental illnesses are members and are responsible for many of the clubhouses activities. Although clubhouses have professional staffs, everyone works together, and the emphasis is on mutual support in an informal atmosphere. Services may include vocational, educational, housing, and advocacy services.

Consumer-run centers are often drop-in centers that are managed by consumers for consumers. They may have self-help programs and self-help groups as well.

Psychosocial rehabilitation programs may provide vocational services, supported education services, social and recreational programs, and personal support for independent living.

Housing Housing programs provide various forms of housing, depending on a person's ability to live independently. Housing options range from fully supervised group homes, to board-and-care homes that provide meals and care, to independent living situations in which minimal supervision is provided on a weekly or monthly basis. Halfway houses are transitional housing programs that provide 24-hour supervision, and some staff help to the residents with personal chores, hygiene, and other activities.

Group homes are long-term housing facilities that usually provide 24-hour supervision, medication monitoring, and staff help to carry out the activities of daily living. Board-and-care homes offer daily meals, dispensation of medications, and minimal staff supervision. Supervised apartments are usually several apartments located within the same complex and are supervised by a staff member who also lives in the complex. Supervision intensity varies depending on the needs of the residents. Supported housing and satellite apartments assist people to live wherever they choose within the community and receive whatever level of support they need to remain independent.

Section 8 Housing, a federal housing and urban development program, is a federally subsidized housing program for people with low incomes. Those who qualify pay a fixed percentage of their income for housing.

Employment The Department of Vocational Rehabilitation (DVR) is the federal agency that provides vocational services at a state level. The agency's goal is to help people with disabilities to return to work. Although most of its caseloads are people with physical disabilities, some programs work very successfully with people with psychiatric disabilities.

Transitional employment programs, often located in clubhouses or similar agencies, place people in temporary jobs to give them a limited employment experience. Two people may share a job, and staff members help with training and emotional support.

Supported employment places people in competitive jobs in the community. A job coach helps individuals learn job skills and adjust to the work environment. These services might be available through a mental health center or a vocational training agency.

Education   Some mental health agencies provide educational services that include general equivalency diploma preparation or remedial classes to upgrade skills in reading, math, and writing. A few programs provide support service that help people return to postsecondary education, but this is the exception rather than the rule. Some hospital programs provide adult education classes in the hospital.

SUMMARY

Although many advances have been made in medications and in the treatment of mental illness, there is still much to learn. Even more important is the necessity for a range and a depth of services based on a philosophy that supports recovery and assists people to live independently and to return to work or school.

REFERENCES

American Psychiatric Association (APA). (1993). *Psychiatric medications: Let's talk about facts.* Washington, DC: Author.

Collier, T. (1993, April 26). The stigma of mental illness. *Newsweek*, 16.

Neugeboren, J. (1997). *Imagining Robert, my brother, madness and survival: A memoir.* New York: William Morrow & Co., Inc.

Physician's Desk Reference (52nd ed.). (1998). Montvale, NJ: Medical Economics.

Risser, P. (1992). An empowering journey. *The Journal of the California Alliance for the Mentally Ill, 3*(2), 38–39.

St. Dennis, C. (1996, June 7). *Psychotropic medications: New drug update.* Paper presented at the Washington Behavioral Healthcare Conference, Yakima, WA.

Stroul, B. (1988). Community support systems for persons with long-term mental illness: A conceptual framework. *Psychosocial Rehabilitation Journal, 11*(3), 9–26.

Psychiatric Disability
Services and the Law

We regret that the effect of your present health condition upon you as a person and upon the college community requires that you receive immediate medical attention during which time you will be placed on medical leave of absence. You are hereby withdrawn. . . . This action is supported by the professional judgment of appropriate college officials as in your best interest at this time. (Pavela, 1985, p. 2)

As a society we must understand disability in order to successfully address discrimination because it often occurs without malice or forethought, it is simply the result of misunderstanding. (Wilkinson & Dresden, 1997, p. 43)

Many people with a diagnosis of mental illness have attempted to return to college after the initial phase of their disorder. Their reception has been mixed, depending on both the attitudes of the staff and the perceived mission of the institution. Responses have ranged from open acceptance to veiled hostility. Although Section 504 of the Rehabilitation Act of 1973 (PL 93-112) prohibits discrimination based on disability, many institutions that receive federal funds have ignored or misinterpreted the statute's meaning when dealing with people with psychiatric disabilities.

With the passage of the Americans with Disabilities Act (ADA) of 1990 (PL 101-336), however, the rights of people with psychiatric disabilities came forcefully to the fore. Many postsecondary institutions had to rethink their policies and procedures and adjust their attitudes. As a result of the ADA, it became more difficult to ignore individuals with psychiatric disabilities or to limit their access to resources on campus, to dismiss them solely on psychiatric grounds, or to deny them admission solely on the basis of their mental illness diagnosis. Since the passage of both Section 504 and the ADA, there has been an ongoing effort to clarify postsecondary policies and practices related to students with disabilities.

This chapter highlights some of the major areas of controversy in postsecondary education that occurred with the passage of Section 504 and the ADA. Several relevant disputes that have arisen in the courts or in the federal Department of Education Office for Civil Rights (OCR) are cited to illustrate situations requiring legal action. These examples are not meant to serve as legal advice or as a definitive interpretation of the laws. They are meant to shed light on the ongoing processes of balancing the rights of the individual with disabilities with the resources and responsibilities of postsecondary institutions.

SECTION 504 AND THE
AMERICANS WITH DISABILITIES ACT

Section 504, enacted in 1973, was designed to give equal opportunities to people with disabilities who sought participation in institutions that received federal funds. The ADA, passed in 1990, expanded the scope of Section 504 to include other public and private entities and brought further attention to Section 504's intent. Title II of the ADA was written to incorporate the language of Section 504 and the case law under it. According to Wilkinson and Dresden (1997), Title II is interpreted, for the most part, to be consistent with Section 504. Section 504 and Title II of the ADA read,

> No otherwise qualified handicapped individual . . . shall, solely by reason of his handicap, be excluded from the participation in, be denied the benefits of, or be subjected to discrimination under any program or activity receiving Federal financial assistance. (cited in Jarrow, n.d., p. 2)

The Language and Intent of the Legislation

Both Section 504 and the ADA used similar terms to define the language and intent of the legislation. In order to qualify as *disabled*, one must have (Section 504 used the word "handicapped")

1) A physical or mental impairment that substantially limits one or more of the major life activities of an individual, 2) a record of such an impairment, or 3) to be regarded as having such an impairment. (§ 35.104)

It is important to note that not all individuals with impairments resulting from a disability are covered under the disability label. The impairments must be severe enough to result in a substantial limitation of one or more major life activities. *Major life activities* are defined as "functions such as caring for one's self, performing manual tasks, walking, seeing, hearing, speaking, breathing, learning, and working" (45 C.F.R. § 84.3[j][2][ii], cited in Pavela, 1985, p. 3). The appendix issued by the Equal Employment Opportunity Commission (EEOC) stated that major life activities are those that "the average person in the general population can perform with little or no difficulty" (42 Fed. Reg. 22, 685, cited in Wilkinson & Dresden, 1997, p. 4).

The intent of both Section 504 and the ADA was to make it illegal to deny admission to college programs and services to students with disabilities if they are otherwise qualified. The laws aimed to include people with psychiatric disabilities with other groups of individuals with disabilities. *Mental impairment* was specifically included in the regulations and cited "any mental or psychological disorder" such as "emotional or mental illness" (45 C.F.R. § 84.3[j][2][i][B], cited in Pavela, 1985, p. 3). The ADA defined a mental impairment as "a physiological disorder or condition . . . affecting one of more of the following body systems: neurological, musculoskeletal . . . special sense organs" (§ 35.104).

It is important to note that the ADA (§ 35.104) also stated that a person qualifies as "disabled" if he or she is regarded as having a physical or mental impairment that, although it does not substantially limit major life activities, is treated as a limitation or an impairment that substantially limits these activities as a result of others' attitudes. Prior to receiving services under the ADA, students must meet eligibility requirements that include verification of the disability and need. It is the responsibility of students to document this information.

Another critical idea of Section 504 and the ADA was the term *otherwise qualified. Qualified*, in the context of education, was defined as "an individual who meets the academic and technical standards requisite to admission or participation in the recipient's education program or activity" (45 C.F.R. § 84.3, App. A at 299, cited in Pavela, 1985, p. 3). The ADA defined a *qualified individual with a disability* as

> An individual with a disability who, with or without reasonable modifications to rules, policies, or practices, the removal of architectural, communication, or transportation barriers, or the provision of auxiliary aids and services, meets the essential eligibility requirements for the receipt of services or the participation in programs or activities provided by a public entity. (§ 35.104)

In a 1979 U.S. Supreme Court case, *Southeastern Community College v. Davis,* the term *otherwise qualified* was defined as an individual who can "meet all of the program requirements in spite of" (cited in Jarrow, n.d., p. 27) his or her disability. *Southeastern Community College v. Davis* involved a student with a hearing impairment who was denied admission into a nursing program because admitting her would have required substantial modifications to the program. The student, however, was not able to meet all the requirements of the program in spite of her impairment. The case not only defined *otherwise qualified* but also made it clear that educational institutions do not have to substantially modify their programs to allow people with disabilities to participate (Pavela, 1985).

A further clarification of the term *otherwise qualified for postsecondary education* is relevant here. According to Kincaid (1994), a student must meet both technical and academic standards of an institution for admission. Technical standards are "all nonacademic admission criteria that are essential to participation in the program in question" (34 C.F.R., Part 104, Appendix A, paragraph [5], cited in Kincaid, 1994, p. 2). Depending on the program, these standards might include physical or mental health requirements. Although students may meet the academic standards, Titles II and III of the ADA refer to the rights of an institution to exclude an individual from participation in its program of activities for health and safety reasons (Appendix A, 28 C.F.R. § 35.104 [qualified individual with disability]; 28 C.F.R. § 36.208 [direct threat], cited in Kincaid, 1994, p. 2).

COMPLIANCE

Every college or university is required to have made provisions for the implementation of Section 504 and the ADA, usually through the Disability Services (DS) Office. This office, or the individual appointed to coordinate the institution's efforts to comply with disability law, has the ongoing responsibility of ensuring that the institution practices non-discriminatory policies and procedures when supporting students with disabilities.

A set of grievance procedures must be available to students for resolving complaints. If a student believes he or she has been unlawfully discriminated against, the student should contact the ADA coordinator for information about the institution's grievance procedures. The student also can file a complaint with the OCR. Information about the disability coordinator and his or her function should be readily available in application packets and student handbooks.

Grievance procedures need to be established and in place so that institutions can respond in a timely manner to requests for accommodations. The requests are usually processed through the DS Office or a designated person who provides disability services. If the compliance office does not respond to a student's needs, the student can file a complaint with the OCR. However, in the suit of *Brown v. Washington University* (1990), the court ruled that a student should not have to file suit against a university for noncompliance with Section 504 (Jarrow, n.d.). The ruling stated that institutions were expected to be proactive in meeting the needs of their students with disabilities.

DOCUMENTATION

In order to level the playing field for students with disabilities, an accommodation may be requested. An *accommodation* is a "modification to academic requirements as necessary to ensure that such requirements do not discriminate against students with disabilities, or have the effect of excluding students solely on the basis of disability" (Jarrow, n.d., p. 16). It is the student's responsibility to request an accommodation and to do so in a timely manner. In addition, accommodations must be accompanied by documentation that states that the impairment substantially limits one or more major life activities. Institutions are responsible for accommodating only known disabilities.

Institutions vary widely on what constitutes proper documentation. *Guckenberger v. Boston University (BU)* (1997) highlighted this controversy. BU had modified its policies, requesting new documentation every 3 years for students with learning disabilities. Guckenberger contended that the diagnostic evaluations were time consuming and expensive. The lawsuit further contended that BU had made the procedures for requesting accommodations overly bureaucratic and burdensome ("Judge's Scathing Decision," 1997). BU lost, and the university was required to reconsider its policy.

The Examinations and Courses section of the ADA stated that "requests for documentation must be reasonable and must be limited to the need for the modification or aid requested" (§ 36.309). Documentation, therefore, should not be required to go beyond what is needed to establish the existence of a disability or an accommodation.

Wilkinson and Dresden (1997) stated that verification of psychological disabilities should be relatively simple and straightforward. In support of this assertion, they cited the ADA: "Appropriate documentation might include a letter from a physician or other professional, or evidence of a prior diagnosis of accommodation, such as eligibility for a special education program" (§ 36.309). For the most part, documentation from preexisting medical records should be adequate. The scope of the information requested should be limited to what is necessary for the purposes of making accommodations. Additional, unnecessary inquiries should not be made.

The documentation of the disability should also demonstrate why the requested accommodation is necessary. The OCR issued a Letter of Findings regarding Cumberland Community College's denial to offer accommodations to a student with disabilities (16 NDLR 418, cited in Wilkinson & Dresden, 1997). The college denied the requested accommodation to a student because the psychological evaluation that was submitted for verification, which documented the student's memory and cognitive disabilities, did not demonstrate that it was necessary to accommodate the disability. Much discussion also has ensued about the OCR's letter regarding who is responsible for appropriate documentation. Here again, the answer is found in Section 36.309, which states that the applicant may be required to bear the cost of providing such documentation.

CONFIDENTIALITY

Some staff members at educational institutions believe that the more information they can gather, the better. Their motives are most often reasonable: to better understand the student and his or her psychiatric disability. Many institutions ask for or require that the student sign release-of-information forms so that staff members can obtain the student's case records.

Case records may contain clinical and treatment information as well as comments from mental health and hospital staff. However, most staff members in DS offices have not had clinical instruction in mental disorders and may make incorrect interpretations about the data. Mental health providers may not be fully sensitive to the rights of the student in terms of confidentiality and may enter inappropriate information into the student's records.

Individuals using the mental health system have been instructed to tell their life stories to doctors, therapists, and therapy groups in their hospital or treatment programs. They are accustomed to having professionals know their clinical and intervention histories. A request for their case histories may not seem like a violation of privacy to them, because it is what they are used to. However, it is important that both the student and the staff at the institution understand how much information is sufficient and when the student's right to privacy is being violated.

Section 504, the ADA, and the Canadian Charter of Rights and Freedoms Act of 1985 provide protection from discrimination based on disability. Included within all three statutes are rules regarding the confidential treatment of disability-related information. Disability-related information must be treated as medical information and must be handled as such. It should be collected and maintained on separate forms and kept in secure files with limited access. It can be shared only within the institutional community with the student's permission or if there is a compelling reason to do so.

To protect the confidentiality of student files, faculty members should not have access to records. They do not need to know the specifics of a student's disability, nor do they need to see actual documentation, including test scores or the names and dates of the person providing such documentation. In general, shared information is limited to informing faculty members that the student has a verified disability and has a need for accommodation (Jarrow, n.d.). Although the Family Educational Rights and Privacy Act of 1974 (PL 93-180), also known as the Buckley Amendment, provided faculty members with the right to see educational information in institutional files for students with whom they work, the act exempts disability records (Association on Higher Education and Disability, 1996). Issues of confidentiality are particularly important for students with psychiatric disabilities because of the stigma associated with those disabilities.

ADMISSION

One of the reasons it was necessary to establish laws guaranteeing equal access to postsecondary institutions for individuals with disabilities is that they were often denied this right. One way that institutions used to exclude people with psychiatric disabilities was to determine through preadmission inquiry that they had a disability and then to maintain separate eligibility criteria for them. However, both preadmission inquiry and separate eligibility criteria are illegal. The ADA stated that

A public entity shall not impose or apply eligibility criteria that screen out or tend to screen out an individual with a disability or any class of individuals with disabilities from fully and equally enjoying any service, program, or activity, unless such criteria can be shown to be necessary for the provision of services, program, or activity being authored. (§ 35.130[8], cited in Wilkson & Dresden, 1997, p. 17)

Typically, a school may not make preadmission inquiries regarding a disability. There have been court cases as well as rulings by the OCR on policies related to admission. For instance, Glendale Community College (Glendale, California) was required to submit a corrective plan to the OCR after a student claimed she was denied admission because of her disability. Glendale's admission forms asked applicants if they have any disability or handicap ("Stay Away from Preadmission," 1995). Pennsylvania State University used to make preadmission inquiries of students it suspected of having emotional or behavior problems. When the university received an application or inquiry from someone who had been incarcerated or who had a history of emotional or behavior problems, the application was put on "hold." These students were then required to release medical records, to have a personal interview, and to provide a psychological evaluation or a comprehensive diagnostic report. The OCR found the university to be in violation of Section 504 regulations (Case No. 03-91-2020, 1991, Region III, cited in Kincaid, 1994, pp. 3–4).

A 1981 case at the University of Colorado (U.S. Court of Appeals for the Tenth Circuit in Pushkin, 1981, cited in Pavela, 1985) addressed the issue of admission to a university program. Although the student in this case did not have psychiatric disabilities, the ruling would most likely apply. The case involved a student who was rejected from a residency program at the university because he had multiple sclerosis and used a wheelchair. His interview ratings for admission were too low because the interviewing panel believed that the psychological impact of his disability would be problematic both for himself and for the individuals with whom he would work. The court ruled in the student's favor, saying that the low rating of the admissions committee was based on incorrect assumptions and faulty information about the nature of the disability.

There are several exceptions to gathering information about a student's disability. Inquiries may be made if a school has been cited for past violations and is trying to increase the number of students with disabilities who attend the school. A school also may make an inquiry if it is trying to document its compliance to restore appropriations of a federally assisted program that relates to funding for special groups of individuals ("Stay Away from Preadmission," 1995).

READMISSION

Readmission to college after a leave of absence can be fraught with controversy. *Doe v. New York University (NYU)* (1981) stated that the NYU Medical School had the right to deny readmission to a student who had a history of psychiatric problems. The student had misrepresented herself in the admissions process, and the court wrote that there was a substantial risk of the illness reoccurring, particularly given the nature of the stresses associated with medical training (Pavela, 1985).

Kincaid (1994) cited three cases regarding conditional readmission. In the first case, Skagit Valley College was found to be in violation of Section 504 and the ADA when it refused to readmit a student who had exhibited disruptive behavior (4 NDLR ¶ 71 [1993]). The dean required the student to provide documentation that she would no longer be disruptive and could benefit from returning to school. After receiving the requested documentation, the dean requested further verification and solicited information from the student's health care providers. Based on this information, the dean denied her readmittance. The OCR stated that after receiving the proper documentation from the student's health care providers, the dean was in violation of Section 504 and the ADA for requiring more additional assurances.

In the second case, the OCR upheld Eastern Carolina University's requirement that a student must agree to certain conditions for readmission (Case No. 04-91-2129 [1991], Region IV, cited in Kincaid, 1994). Because of the student's history of violent behavior (e.g., theft, suicide threats), he was required to agree to a set of conditions that included psychotherapy and medication management, monthly reports from his physician, and notification of any destabilization of his condition or the provision of emergency medical services.

The third case also upheld a college's requirement for conditions placed on a student's readmission (Case No. 01-90-2006 [1990], Region I, cited in Kincaid, 1994). A student with a bipolar disorder was required by Bowdoin College (Brunswick, Maine) to continue his medication, attend therapy, and provide written evidence of successful treatment.

ACCOMMODATIONS

Providing the accommodations requested by a student is where law and policy meet practice. At this juncture, the needs of the students must be balanced with the responsibilities and resources of the institution. Accommodations are sometimes necessary to ensure that a student with a disability is given equal opportunities to succeed and that nondiscriminatory practices are in place. However, the provision of accommodations may require that institutions allocate their resources away from other programs or services.

In one of the earliest cases to address the issue of providing accommodations, *Barnes v. Converse College* (1977), the court found that an institution could not deny accommodations strictly on the basis of cost alone. This case dealt with the provision of interpreter services to a student with a hearing impairment but is often cited in situations in which the cost of auxiliary aids and services are at issue (Jarrow, n.d.).

In determining the accommodations that should be given, it may be important to differentiate between what is necessary and what is desired by the student. Some deference should be given to the individual's preferred modification, but the institution is not required to provide the best technology that is available. The final criterion is whether the accommodation provided is sufficient to ensure nondiscrimination.

Wynne v. Tufts University School of Medicine (1991) formulated a test for determining whether an academic institution performed an adequate search for possible accommodations:

> If the institution submits undisputed facts demonstrating that the relevant officials within the institution considered alternative means, their feasibility, cost and effect on the academic program, and came to either lowering academic standards or requiring substantial program alteration, the court could rule as a matter of law that the institution had met its duty of seeking reasonable accommodation. (Wilkinson & Dresden, 1997, pp. 23–24)

There have been a number of cases to determine what is a reasonable accommodation (see Chapter 5). The following sections review several accommodations and the relevant court cases that apply to each.

Tutors

The OCR regards tutorial assistance as a personal service (Rancho Santiago Community College, cited in Jarrow, n.d.). The OCR indicated that tutorial services are personal services and are not required as an auxiliary aid or service under Section 504. Institutions are required to provide only those tutorial services to students with disabilities that they provide to students without disabilities. However, if a college generally offers tutors to all of its students, then students with disabilities are entitled to equal access. The college may place parameters around the service. For example, tutors may not have to read and interpret a textbook for a student.

Home-Based Instruction

A student at Cabrillo Community College (Cabrillo, California) requested home tutoring for an entire semester because of multiple chemical sensitivities. One of the classes for which the home tutoring was requested included a laboratory component. The OCR ruled that a college's responsibility to provide auxiliary aids did not extend beyond the college's boundaries and that home study might be considered a service that is for personal use or study, similar to tutoring services. The OCR also ruled that to grant the request would have substantially altered the program (Case No. 09-96-2150 [1996] ORC, Region IX, 1996, cited in Kincaid, 1996).

Assistive Devices

Many students with psychiatric disabilities find a tape recorder to be an effective aid to their learning. Some instructors, however, are uncomfortable having their classes recorded. Tape recorders are one of the accommodations specifically mentioned in Section 504 as a means of ensuring full participation in education programs or activities. The faculty's right to privacy does not override the student's right to accommodation, and instructors cannot forbid a student from bringing a tape recorder to class (Jarrow, n.d.).

Testing

Testing modifications are one of the most controversial accommodations. A number of situations regarding testing have come to the attention of the courts or the OCR. These situations have involved not only educational institutions but also testing entities, such as the Education Testing Service or other services that provide exams for licenses or certifications. Both Section 504 and the ADA require that tests be administered in a nondiscriminatory manner. Therefore, testing modifications should be made unless the institution or the testing authority can show that the modification would fundamentally alter the test. Section 504 is very clear on the issue of testing accommodations. It requires that covered entities should not use

> Any test or criterion . . . that has a disproportionate adverse effect on . . . individuals with disabilities, except when the test or criterion has been validated as a predictor of success in the education program or activity inquisition, and . . . alternate tests that have a less disproportionate, adverse effect are not . . . available." (§ 104.42, cited in Wilkinson & Dresden, 1997, pp. 9–10)

However, the U.S. Supreme Court found that Section 504 does not require an institution to lower or make substantial modifications to its standards to accommodate an individual with a disability (*Southeastern Community College v. Davis*, 1979, cited in Pavela, 1985).

Title III of the ADA, which covers private entities as well as federally supported institutions, specifically prohibits discrimination by any private entity that offers examinations or courses related to licensing, certification, or credentials for secondary or postsecondary education, professional, or trade purposes. Specifically, Section 36.309(1) requires the following:

> The examination is selected and administered so as best to assure that, when the examination is administered to an individual with a disability that impairs sensory, manual, or speaking skills, the examination results accurately reflect the individual's aptitude or achievement level or whatever other factor the examination purports to measure, rather than reflecting the individual's impaired sensory, manual, or speaking skills (except where those are the factors the examination purports to measure). (cited in Wilkinson & Dresden, 1997, p. 11)

These special exams should also be offered and administered as frequently as other examinations in locations that are equally convenient. Facilities offering these examinations should be "accessible to individuals with disabilities," or the testing entity should make "alternative accessible arrangements" (Title III, § 36.203).

One of the most common requests for accommodations has been additional time for testing. Initially, the Educational Testing Service placed ceilings on the amount of extended time given for exams based on the category of the candidate's disability. However, the OCR struck down this policy and stated that the accommodation must be based on the individual needs of the candidate, not on his or her disability category (Kincaid, 1994a). It has been argued that additional time for tests gives the student with a disability an advantage over other test takers. It is interesting to note that research has shown otherwise. Runyan (1991), in a study at the University of California, indicated that extended time makes a significant impact on the performance of students with disabilities but does not have a significant impact on the performance of students without disabilities.

Wynne v. Tufts University School of Medicine (1991, cited in Wilkinson & Dresden, 1997) examined the issue of possible discriminatory issuance of a multiple-choice test to a student with a learning disability. The student claimed the test was discriminatory and requested an alternative testing format. The court found in favor of the medical school because it claimed the format was necessary to test the student's ability to quickly synthesize information. The school was able to demonstrate that no reasonable alternative could be provided. The court also found that Section 504 was not intended "to eliminate academic or professional requirements that measure proficiency in analyzing written information by attaining a passing score on a multiple choice test" (Wilkinson & Dresden, 1997, p. 12). A further point was that a university must consider requests for accommodations on an individual basis (Jarrow, n.d.). *The United States v. South Carolina* (1977, cited in Wilkinson & Dresden, 1997) found that the state had "the right to adopt academic requirements and to use written achievement tests designed and validated to disclose the minimum amount of knowledge necessary to effective teaching" (Wilkinson & Dresden, 1997, pp. 12–13)

Another point of contention in terms of accommodations is who bears the responsibility for the expense of the accommodation. Wilkinson and Dresden stated the following: "Under both 504 and the ADA the obligation to provide access to testing and educational opportunities extends to the point that an 'undue financial or administrative burden is imposed an on institution'" (1997, p. 29). They suggested three criteria for determining whether there is a burden imposed:

1. Nature and cost of the action
2. The overall financial resources available to the program
3. The impact of providing the aid or service on the program

By using these guidelines, an institution may not be required to provide an accommodation if it can demonstrate that an alternative means of testing was considered, that the alternative means were not feasible because of the cost and/or effect on the academic program, and that the alternatives would either lower academic standards or require substantial program alteration.

Previous rulings about who bears the cost of accommodations stated that a student was required to apply for Vocational Rehabilitation services as a condition of receiving accommodations from a college. However, the OCR stated that such a requirement violates Section 504 and the ADA (Kincaid, 1996). It is inappropriate for a college to require that a student go through the considerable effort to apply for Vocational Rehabilitation services when students without disabilities are not required to do so (Kincaid, 1996).

Yet another issue regarding testing modification pertains to the time it takes an institution to respond to student requests for accommodations. If a student requests an accommodation and the institutions or agency takes the matter under consideration, the student is entitled to a timely response. Policies regarding approval or denial for accommodations should be designed to allow time for an appeal. In

Glass v. New York State Board of Bar Examiners (1996), the attorneys representing a bar applicant were able to obtain a temporary restraining order so that the applicant could take the bar examination while the issue was being settled.

Controversy has also arisen about the validity of altered test formats. Often the testing authorities flag the results of alternative test formats, which puts prospective institutions on notice that the applicant is a person with a disability. The Educational Testing Service puts an asterisk on test scores, which denotes that the test was taken in a nonstandard method (e.g., extended time, braille tests, recorded tests). This type of policy is permitted, but institutions are required to consider other factors in the admission process ("SAT Scores," 1995).

Substitutions and Waivers

Historically, people with disabilities have been screened out of certain professions or trades because it was assumed that their disabilities might interfere with the practice of that profession or trade. In providing the education and training necessary to succeed in a particular profession, it is important to look at the body of knowledge that is required, how it is imparted, and how it is tested (Wilkinson & Dresden, 1997). Section 504 and the ADA do not prohibit institutions from establishing specific criteria for certain academic programs. The laws are not intended to interfere with legitimate academic requirements. However, substitutions or waivers that do not alter the necessary body of knowledge or skills that are required should be considered as possible accommodations.

Section 504 states that modifications may include substitution of specific courses required for the completion of degree requirements. When requirements have been challenged, the courts look at how essential the program or testing requirements are to the program. If the waiver of a requirement would cause a fundamental alteration in the program, then it probably does not have to be waived. It is the responsibility of the institution to show that a requirement is essential to a given course of study and that making a substitution would substantially alter the curriculum for the student (Jarrow, n.d.).

Foreign language classes have been waived by many colleges and universities when it has been demonstrated that they were not necessary to the academic program in which the student with mental illness was enrolled. Another frequently requested modification—math—is more difficult to waive. Math is often essential to the body of knowledge required to practice a particular profession or trade.

In evaluating whether a college has upheld its obligation to provide accommodations in the area of waiving courses, the OCR applied these questions to a case at Bennett College (Greensboro, North Carolina):

1. Did the student provide adequate notices of his or her need for academic adjustment?
2. Was an academic adjustment necessary?
3. Was an appropriate adjustment provided?
4. Was the adjustment that was provided effective? ("Waive course requirements," 1995, p. 5)

The case under question at Bennett College involved a student who asked that a language requirement be waived because he had severe panic disorder and agoraphobia. The university responded to the OCR's requirements by offering the student an option of taking one of three languages under independent study, providing him with a tutor, or providing him with assistance in identifying faculty members who would be understanding of the disorder should he decide to take the course on campus. He also was given an opportunity to enroll in a special learning program designed to teach concentration and memory skills techniques ("Waive course requirements," 1995).

Special Programs

Colleges and universities often provide special programs for individuals with disabilities or other groups of individuals. The programs may be designed to address a certain need or interest of the students. In selecting participants for the special programs, the institutions may ask questions about the person's disability to ensure that the student qualifies for the program (Kincaid, 1994). For example, a college may offer a special program for people with learning disabilities, and in order for a student to qualify, he or she must have a documented learning disability.

Disruptive Students

Having students with mental disorders who may be disruptive on campus is an area of particular controversy in postsecondary institutions. There are still many misconceptions about the nature of mental illness and the people who have this diagnosis. The media have portrayed people with mental illness as violent and dangerous although numerous studies show that they are not more violent or dangerous than the general population (Monahan, 1992; Monahan & Arnold,

1996; Mulvey, 1994). In fact, they are often the victims of crimes rather than the perpetrators.

However, the idea persists that students with a psychiatric disability are the most disruptive students on campus. A study (Parton, 1993) conducted on four campuses of the California Community College System addressed this issue directly. In implementing special programs for students with psychiatric disabilities, the study found that the students at service sites were not disruptive. The colleges also provided emergency crisis intervention services and found them underutilized (Parton, 1993). Along the same line, in one of the first references to address this topic, Pavela wrote, "Educators often overstate the risk of liability for failing to protect students from the violent acts of others, or from self-destructive behavior" (1985, p. 35).

Despite these facts, an uneasiness persists among many college staff members who are unfamiliar with working with people with mental illness. This uneasiness manifests itself in many ways, but perhaps one of the most common is that instructors are reluctant to confront students with mental illness in their classes about their behavior. The law is very clear, however, about the students' responsibility to conduct themselves in a manner consistent with institutional policy.

In 1977, the Attorney General of the United States published an opinion pertaining to Section 504, which stated that the law would not require unrealistic accommodations if a person's behavior was unduly disruptive to others (43 Op. Atty. Gen., Nov. 12, 1977). A related analysis was released by the U.S. Department of Health, Education and Welfare (since renamed the U.S. Department of Health and Human Services), which said that an institution could hold a drug addict or alcoholic to the same standards of performance and behaviors even if the unsatisfactory behavior is related to the person's mental impairment (45 C.F.R. § 84, 1983, cited in Pavela, 1985). Pavela added that presumably the same standards would hold for any individual with a comparable mental impairment. Rulings during the 1990s have upheld this opinion.

In 1993, Western Michigan University's decision to suspend a student with paranoid schizophrenia from classes and to prohibit the student from entering the campus was upheld by the OCR even though the student's behavior might have resulted from her disability (3 NDLR ¶ 267 [Region V]; cited in Kincaid, 1994). The student had engaged in behavior that disrupted university activities and was viewed as disturbing and threatening by students, faculty, and staff. The university's decision was made on the basis of their observation of the student and the opinion of the psychiatric professionals involved in the situation.

In 1990, the OCR upheld a decision (Case No. 05-90-2019 [Region V], cited in Kincaid, 1994) made by Western State University to recommend that a student withdraw from school so she could receive treatment. The student had frequent outbursts and was disruptive during classes. She also was observed to be in a psychotic state in her dormitory. When the director of counseling met with the student, he found her to be incoherent. OCR found that the actions of the university were based on a legitimate concern for the welfare of the other students as well as the faculty at the university.

In 1992, the OCR supported the University of California's request that a student with cerebral palsy undergo psychological evaluation because of inappropriate behavior, including allegations of sexual harassment (Case No. 09-91-2138 [Region IX], cited in Kincaid, 1994). The OCR found that the Hasting Law School's actions were consistent with carrying out its responsibility to aid the student in having a productive educational experience.

These cases demonstrate that students on campus, regardless of their disabilities, can and should be held to the same standards of behavior as students without disabilities. To hold these students accountable to other standards is to support the notion that they are, in fact, "different." Correspondingly, these students need to be treated with the same respect and dignity afforded to all students. Due process that takes into consideration confidentiality and the nature of the disability must be in place through the student code of conduct. If a student cannot or will not meet reasonable institutional standards, it might be the ground for exclusion or withdrawal (Pavela, 1985).

Psychiatric Withdrawal

In a seminal text entitled *The Dismissal of Students with Mental Disorders: Legal Issues, Policy Considerations and Alternative Responses,* Pavela (1985) wrote about the existing policies at many colleges and universities prior to the passage of the ADA. He described a survey of 123 higher education institutions that revealed a majority of them had provisions for the mandatory withdrawal of students who had mental, emotional, or behavior disorders. These mandatory withdrawals included students who had also threatened or attempted suicide. Once a student was identified as fitting one or more of the categories discussed previously, he or she was withdrawn for "medical" or "psychiatric" reasons. The withdrawal was often stated as being in the student's best interest. Such policies denied the student's due process rights and were often in violation of Section 504.

Pavela (1985) suggested that instead of psychiatric withdrawal, an institution should rely on a well-formulated student code of conduct. A code of conduct allows two things to happen. First, it separates the student from his or her diagnosis. Regardless of a disability, students must conform to institutional standards of behavior in order to be admitted or to remain in school. A thoughtful student code of conduct sets the label of mental illness aside and looks only at students' behavior.

Second, a code of conduct gives all parties a standard on which to judge behavior and, if a code should be violated, a process for managing the behavior. It provides for prescribed and formal procedures in which due process can be followed. It removes the arbitrary decisions that can occur with a psychiatric withdrawal and the possible violation of students' rights.

SUMMARY

Section 504 and the ADA guarantee students with psychiatric disabilities equal access to the education environment. Federal laws are being explained more clearly through the litigation process. As these laws continue to be challenged and explicated, the role of the educational institution and its staff will become more clear. Over time, a realistic assessment of the costs and benefits of these landmark legislations will be made. As of 1998, the guarantees provided to the students have already opened up new opportunities that were formerly not available. In terms of personal benefits, for a group of individuals that many had written off as lost forever, the outcomes have been immeasurable in advances in productivity, quality of life, and self-esteem.

REFERENCES

Americans with Disabilities Act (ADA) of 1990, PL 101-336, 42 U.S.C. §§ 12101 *et seq.*

Association on Higher Education and Disability. (1996). Columbus, OH: Author.

Barnes v. Converse College, 436 F. Supp. 635 (D.S.C. 1977).

Brown v. Washington University, No. 88-1907, C-5 (Mo. Ct. App., 1990).

Family Educational Rights and Privacy Act of 1974, PL 93-180, 20. U.S.C. §§ 1232g *et seq.*

Glass v. New York State Board of Bar Examiners, N.D. N.Y. Settlement, March, 1996, 8 NDLR)

Guckenberger v. Boston University, 957 F. Supp. 306 (D. Mass. 1997)

Jarrow, J. (n.d.). *Subpart E: The impact of Section 504 on postsecondary education.* Columbus, OH: Association on Higher Education and Disability.

Judges scathing decision may have limited legal impact, but provides guidance relief for disability service office. (1997). *Disability Compliance for Higher Education, 3*(3), 6–7.

Kincaid, J.M. (1994). *A review of case law as applied to students with psychological disabilities in institutions of higher learning.* Barnstead, NH: Author.

Kincaid, J.M. (1996). Recent legal decisions. *Alert, 20*(5), 4.

Parton, D. (1993). Implementation of a systems approach to supported education at four California Community College Model Service Sites. *Psychosocial Rehabilitation Journal, 17*(1), 171–188.

Pavela, G. (1985). *The dismissal of students with mental disorders: Legal issues, policy considerations and alternative responses.* The Higher Education Administration Series. Asheville, NC: College Administration Publications, Inc.

SAT scores may point out disability. (December, 1995). *Disability Compliance for Higher Education, 1*(5), 10.

Stay away from preadmission questions about disabilities. (December, 1995). *Disability Compliance for Higher Education, 1*(5), 10.

Trident Enterprises, Inc. (1992). *A guide to the Americans with Disabilities Act of 1990: A technical assistance resource for California Community College.*

Waive course requirements only when they're not essential to the program. (1995). *Disability Compliance for Higher Education, 1,*(5), 5.

Wilkinson, W., & Dresden, B. (1997, September). *The Americans with Disabilities Act and the Rehabilitation Act of 1973 and their application to educational issues: Proceedings. Symposium on accommodating adults with disabilities in adult education programs.* Paper presented at the 1996 National Association for Adults with Special Learning Needs Conference, New Orleans, LA. Lawrence: Center for Research on Learning, University of Kansas.

5

Providing Accommodations and Services in Educational Settings

One of the greatest needs . . . of persons with a mental illness is for their educators to be educated. (Mosley, 1994, p. 4)

The line between mental health and illness is blurred; much is to be learned from one another across that line. Individual students and the college as a whole benefit from the creation of a community that operates, supports, and actively encourages academic engagement for students experiencing a variety of emotional illnesses. Our understanding of the human condition is enhanced in the educational environments that value diversity of experience and expression and foster, through supportive policy and practice, the intellectual and personal growth of all who work and study within. (Hoffmann & Mastrianni, 1989, p. 21)

With this student population I have learned as much about accepting all aspects of myself as I have about the psychological disabilities with which I have come into contact. I look forward to seeing more and more students coming through the door to meet their own personal challenges. (Cavendor, 1994, p. 12)

College is a bridge from one stage of life to another. In the best of circumstances, it teaches people a profession or trade and prepares them to enter the professional world. Other transitions such as job changes (e.g., promotions, layoffs), children leaving home, divorce, and changes in health are also times when people return to school to upgrade their present skills or to learn new skills. It is no wonder, then, that people with psychiatric disabilities see education as a means of regaining their place in society.

With the onset of a mental illness, people may lose the legitimate roles (e.g., student, worker, family member, friend) that they once held. The loss comes because they are no longer viewed as the same people that they used to be. As with all people with a disability, there has to be a shift. Not only has the person had the experience of the illness, but he or she also must now cope with some changes in functioning. Part of the recovery from a mental disorder, as with any disability, is a reframing of personal identity. Who is this new person with the disability, and what will his or her life be like now? Education is a valuable tool to use during this reframing process.

With deinstitutionalization and improvements in psychotropic medication, people with mental illness are returning to school in record numbers. However, their appearance on campus has sometimes been met with trepidation. Mental illness is still one of the least understood major illnesses. It is enveloped in fear and darkness. In workshops all over the United States, college faculty and staff express similar fears—often cloaked in practical questions: Who is appropriate for college? How do I relate to these students? What if a student becomes violent? The images of psychopathic killers in newspapers and on television screens are almost visible in their eyes.

This chapter addresses the fears associated with mental illness and supports the joys of working with people with a mental disorder. It has been the experience of many college staff that once they got to know students with psychiatric disabilities, their images changed from fear to respect and admiration. It is the intent of this chapter to facilitate this transition.

The questions most frequently asked by college staff about working with individuals with a mental disorder fall into six categories:

1. Who is eligible for college?
2. What problems will students with a mental disorder have on campus?
3. What accommodations are reasonable?
4. What are realistic goals for students with a mental disorder?
5. What skills do I need to work with students with a mental disorder?

6. How can I ensure comfort and safety for both the student and myself?

This chapter answers these questions as they relate to accommodations and services. (See Chapter 6 for a detailed discussion of health and safety issues.) In answering any of these questions, the best advice is to remember that students with psychiatric disabilities are more alike than they are different from students without disabilities. Each is an individual with unique values, abilities, and needs. If a question arises about what to do, the best source of information may be the student.

ELIGIBILITY FOR ADMISSION AND SERVICES

Colleges, universities, and technical skills training programs vary in their admission requirements. According to both Section 504 of the Rehabilitation Act of 1973 (PL 93-112) and the Americans with Disabilities Act (ADA) of 1990 (PL 101-336), a person with a disability is eligible for admission if he or she meets—with or without accommodation—the eligibility requirements of the institution. To be eligible for admission, an individual with a psychiatric disability needs to meet only the eligibility criteria of the program. (See Chapter 4 for further information on eligibility.) If the student meets the eligibility requirements, the next step is to determine whether he or she is eligible for disability services under the law. In order for a person to receive services under Section 504 or the ADA, he or she must have an impairment that substantially limits one or more major life activities. In order to determine if there is an impairment or a verifiable disability, students must present documentation of their diagnoses.

In most instances, a licensed psychiatrist, a psychologist with a Ph.D., or other qualified mental health professionals can provide verification of a psychiatric disability. (Note: The qualifications required to make a mental illness diagnosis may vary from state to state in the United States.) Students also may provide documentation from the Department of Vocational Rehabilitation, from the Department of Mental Health, from the Social Security Administration, or from records available from their high school district or other community agencies. Flexibility in documentation is important, particularly if a college has many nontraditional students.

Documentation of a disability must include the following:

*   Verification of an individual's psychiatric condition

- Dates of registration or treatment, including enrollment and termination dates
- Last date of contact
- How the person's disability/disorder may affect him or her in the academic setting
- The professional's credentials, including license or certification and area of specialization

It is helpful if the information in the documentation also includes a description of the presenting symptoms of the disorder, the kinds of medications being taken and their side effects on the person, and recommendations for academic accommodations and why they are needed. Some mental health professionals may not be familiar with the accommodations that are available and will be unable to provide this information.

In obtaining documentation, it is important to seek information from a licensed professional. If the student is working with several professionals, obtain information based on the student's recommendation from the professional who has the most accurate picture of the student's functioning.

Diagnostic and functional limitation information are necessary for official documentation; recommendations for academic accommodations are optional. A description of how the disorder affects the individual and the side effects of the medication can be of great assistance to the disability services (DS) counselor. In addition, intake is a good time to ask the student whether he or she receives services and whether these service providers may be contacted in certain agreed-on circumstances.

BARRIERS TO STUDENT SUCCESS ON CAMPUS

Because each person is unique, individuals with psychiatric disabilities will bring varied functional limitations to the college environment. There are certain barriers, however, that all students with a mental disorder face that interfere with being successful on campus (Parton, Amada, & Unger, 1991).

Stigma

People with a mental illness are still not widely included in the range of cultures, races, lifestyles, or behaviors that we are encouraged to learn about and accept in our daily lives. There are still people who stage "Not in My Neighborhood" campaigns to prevent people with mental disorders from residing next door to them. There are still college staff who question the appropriateness of having a student with a psychiatric disability in their school or classroom. *Stigma*, a mark of shame or discredit, still haunts individuals who, through no fault of their own, have had a mental illness, and they frequently take on the shame and diminished expectations placed on them by others.

Lack of Opportunities

Medical treatment and therapy are most often the interventions provided to people with a mental illness. Unlike people who have a physical disability, individuals with mental illness seldom receive rehabilitation services to help them regain their skills or learn new skills so they can return to an independent level of functioning and resume as typical a life as possible. If someone has a severe accident and is physically injured, the individual is hospitalized, treated, and given rehabilitative services so he or she can return to his or her usual life activities. However, if someone has a nervous breakdown, or a *psychotic break*, the person is hospitalized, treated, and discharged. Rehabilitation services are often inadequate; if the individual is assisted to return to work, it is often in an entry-level position or as an unskilled laborer. These individuals lose their place in the world of work as well as the personal relationships and sense of worth that accompany meaningful work. Opportunities are lost and regained only with extreme effort.

The Nature of Mental Illness

The complex nature of a mental illness is often a barrier in itself. The disabilities caused by the disorder may result in cognitive or perceptual difficulties. Increased vulnerability to stress and anxiety may make it difficult for an individual to function at the highest level of which he or she is capable. Seeming lethargic, inattentive, restless, or anxious, individuals may appear to be poor students when in fact it is their symptoms or side effects of medication and not their actual intents that are seen. The episodic nature of the illness is also problematic. Students may go through long periods in which they are stable and show few symptoms. At other times, however, the symptoms may become more florid, taking energy away from the task at hand. Some people even have "anniversaries" that remind them of very sad or difficult times and find it difficult to function during these times.

Side Effects of Medication

The medications used to treat mental illness are very powerful and have many residual side effects. In some ways they take away one disability and substitute another. Although the drugs may not diminish intellectual ability, they can make the person so uncomfortable that they have trouble with very simple things, such as sitting still. Because of the medicating effects, a student may be unable to get to an early class. The side effects of the medication may also make it hard to concentrate. In more extreme cases, students may have blurred vision; memory lapses; thirst; agitation; or involuntary movement of hands, feet, or facial muscles. Although many of the new medications are more effective and have fewer side effects than previous drugs, they are still potent and cause changes in a person's bodily functions and how they are able to manage their daily tasks.

STUDENTS' SPECIAL NEEDS ON CAMPUS

There has been little formal research on supported education and people with psychiatric disabilities. In the early 1990s, two studies appeared in the literature that examined the student's functional limitations in the education environment (Parton, 1993; Unger, 1993). Each study asked the students (N = 300) to identify from a list their anticipated problems on campus. Because the lists were different, it is not possible to determine which were the most prevalent problems; but in rough order, they are as follows:

- Applying for financial aid
- Learning/concentration
- Registration
- Selecting classes
- Managing internal distractions
- Relationships
- Taking tests and notes
- Time management

Other problems identified by students included studying, being flexible, staying focused, attending class regularly and on time, making and keeping appointments, planning, asking for help, problem solving in new situations, dealing with forms, parking, being aware of and managing stress, making friends, and talking with authority figures (Parton, Amada, & Unger, 1991). In addition to psychiatric disabilities, 26% of the students also identified one or more physical disabilities (Unger, 1993).

Most problems identified by students are not intellectual. Although students may have had their academic progress interrupted by a mental disorder, most have completed high school (90%), with only a small percentage in special education (17%) (Unger, 1996). The problems encountered are primarily a result of the disabilities of the mental illness and interrupted development. Depending on the age at onset of the illness (usually between 18 and 25 years) and the resulting disability, academic achievement may not be appropriate to the person's age group and intellectual ability. While their classmates were attending college, working, forming relationships, and having a myriad of adolescent and young adult experiences, young adults with mental illness may have been in and out of hospitals and struggling simply to maintain themselves. As they enter their early 30s, many of these individuals are ready to resume their education and try to pick up where they had left off, about 15 years behind their peers (Unger, 1993). They are not unlike other students with disabilities who also often have an inconsistent academic history and difficulties with coping with stress and low self-esteem (Parton, Amada, & Unger, 1991).

Medications and Learning

Although no studies have been done on the effects of psychotropic medication on college functioning, it is generally understood that the medications do not interfere. In Unger's (1997) study, students with psychiatric disabilities who were involved with supported education programs completed 90% of the courses in which they enrolled and maintained a grade point average of 3.3 on a 4-point scale. A 1995 (Wilson, 1995) report on the role of medications in the treatment of individuals with a dual diagnosis of learning disabilities and psychiatric disabilities gives other helpful information. Wilson (1995) stated that antidepressant drugs in general appear to improve one's ability to learn as they reduce the debilitating mood abnormalities that impair the ability to attend, think, and learn. Some antidepressant drugs, such as tricyclics (e.g., Elavil, Tofranil), may improve cognition. Other drugs used to treat bipolar disorder (e.g., Prozac, Paxil, Elavil) do not generally affect learning. The one exception is Tegretol, which seems to have adverse effects on psychomotor performance, memory, and information processing.

Another category of drugs, benzodiazepine, is used as an antianxiety medication and includes Librium, Xanax, and Ativan. These drugs may cause memory problems in the short term; but over time, the effect disappears. However, they can cause drowsiness, occasional dizziness, and unsteadiness, all of which can contribute to problems with alertness and cognition.

Antipsychotic medications for people with thought disorders such as schizophrenia are more problematic. Drugs like Haldol, Thorazine, Navane, and others may improve learning simply because they reduce symptoms. However, there is also evidence that these medications impair cognition and can be highly sedating.

Although there may be general statements one can make about medications, the effects they have on individuals vary. Wilson stated the following:

> Psychotropic drugs have the potential to both improve and disrupt cognition and learning on many different levels. Unfortunately, much of life can improve and disrupt cognition and learning as well. Thus, one cannot usefully determine what effect psychotropic drugs will have on an individual's cognition. Not only is each individual different in respect to how they will react to a particular psychotropic drug, but they are also different with respect to all the other factors that can disrupt cognition. Thus, one cannot assume that a particular psychotropic drug is having one effect, another effect, or no effect on a person's cognition. (1995, p. 9)

Functional limitations for people with psychiatric disabilities are very individualized and may vary over time. It is important to maintain an ongoing dialogue with students to assess their functioning and need for accommodations throughout the school year.

Accommodations and Services

By law, students with a verifiable disability must be given accommodations. However, many colleges and universities provide additional support services to enhance the student's opportunities for success. Others go beyond accommodations and support services and provide classes or programs designed especially to help students with psychiatric disabilities, just as many campuses have developed specific programs for students with learning disabilities. The following subsections discuss accommodations and several types of additional support services.

Accommodations   An *accommodation* is "a modification to academic requirements as necessary to ensure that such requirements do not discriminate against students with disabilities, or have the effect of excluding students solely on the basis of the disability" (Jarrow, n.d., p. 16). This definition is expanded to include

> Modifications as needed in policies, practices, and procedures and for assuring accessibility of examinations and courses . . . all aspects of academic and nonacademic activities including admissions and recruitment, admission to programs, academic adjustments, housing, financial assistance,

physical education and athletics, and counseling. (HEATH Resource Center and Association on Higher Education and Disability, n.d.)

In order for a student to receive an accommodation, he or she must have a verified disability and must request an accommodation. Not all students know what accommodations and services are available or how to gain access to them. In order to facilitate this process, the institution has an obligation to make their services known. In addition, students may need help in determining the functional limitations they will have on a college campus and the effect these limitations will have on their success.

Some of the most common accommodations needed by students, based on an assessment of their functional limitations, include the following:

- Notetaker services in the classroom
- Use of tape recorders in the classrooms
- Books on tape
- Test-taking facilitation, including arrangements, proctoring, and modification of tests and test administration
- Changes in timelines for assignments
- Changes in format or method of completing assignments
- The use of cubicles, headphones, or individual rooms during tests
- Course substitutions or waivers
- Part-time status with extensions of that status as necessary
- Incomplete rather than failing grades if the student needs a medical withdrawal
- Taking beverages to class
- Arrangements to leave and return to class during a class period, as needed
- Changes in seating
- Special parking permits

Support Services   Although support services are not required by law, they often help students remain in school. Support services may be provided by the DS office, or they may be provided by other offices on campus. For example, help with registration may be provided by the Registrar's Office; financial aid assistance may be provided by the Financial Aid Office; and career counseling and job placement may be provided by the Career Opportunities Office or its equivalent. The following are support services that are often very helpful to students with psychiatric disabilities:

- Registration assistance, including priority enrollment assistance
- Assistance in applying for financial aid
- Academic counseling that includes choosing classes that meet individual academic or personal goals with the student's functional limitations in mind
- Counseling, including specialized academic, vocational, personal, and peer counseling services
- Assistance with compiling and consolidating transcripts from other institutions
- Assistance in applying for forgiveness of previous loans because of disability status
- Having a quiet place on campus to relax or rest
- Having someone with whom to check in
- Liaison with campus and community agencies, including referrals and follow-up services
- Supplemental or individualized orientation to the campus
- Goal setting
- Career counseling
- Job placement

Special Classes   Another support service that is very useful to students is special classes that teach basic skills. They may include studying, time management, and test taking. Also helpful are classes on problem-solving strategies, symptom and/or disability management, managing free time, and adult developmental psychology. Special classes also provide a transitional environment in which students can become acclimated to the campus and maintaining a schedule. Some students also need help with social skills, such as making friends and managing their free time on campus; transitional classes may provide friends or acquaintances who can become part of their peer support and social network.

Supported Education Programs   Supported education programs go a step further: Their primary focus is providing services to students with psychiatric disabilities. They have staff who are specifically trained to work with the students and resources available to provide a greater range of services. The College of San Mateo (San Mateo, California) has such a program. (See Chapter 7 for a detailed description of the program.) One of the distinguishing characteristics of this program is its collaboration with other community resources. Other colleges and universities have designated staff that work only with students with psychiatric disabilities. Although the institutions may not have a prescribed program, the services may be more specifically targeted to this group of students.

Medications Changes in the student's medication may require changes in accommodations. Occasionally, students' medications or dosages of medications change. This can be very disruptive and cause unanticipated consequences. As students become more accustomed to being in school, they become more knowledgeable about the effects of the medication on their performance. Many try to keep their medications consistent throughout the semester and try to make changes when they are not in school, if at all possible. Sometimes psychiatrists will prescribe changes, unaware of the effect that they will have on the students.

DS staff and counselors are often in a good position to help students monitor the effects of their medications. Although medication monitoring is the primary responsibility of the students themselves and their mental health services providers, college staff who see the students frequently may notice changes in behavior before the students are aware of the changes. When these changes occur, it is helpful to the student to have feedback, to explore the need for some medication change, or to request a change in an accommodation.

Disclosure and Confidentiality Another issue related to accommodation is disclosure. Many students choose not to disclose their disability. Such a choice may be influenced by the culture of the environment, which can be demonstrated by the printed materials related to student services and how prominent psychological or psychiatric disorders are noted. It may also be influenced by reports from other students about discriminatory practices by instructors. Fear of disclosure may also come from the student's lack of understanding about his or her legal rights (Dougherty et al., 1996).

Students also may be influenced by their fear that confidentiality will be violated. To avoid formally disclosing, some students go directly to an academic instructor for an accommodation. This process can be somewhat capricious, depending on the personality of the instructor and the student's skills. In most instances, it is to the student's advantage to disclose to the DS staff; however, in most instances, in order for students to do so, the college must create an atmosphere of respect and trust. By law, disability-related information should be treated as medical information and handled under the same strict rules of confidentiality as is other medical information. It should be collected and maintained on separate forms, kept in secure files, and shared only when there is a compelling reason. All students are not aware of the rules designed for their privacy or fear a violation of their privacy rights.

Another reason for not disclosing is that students may not want special help. A former student said the following:

Consumers, in general, don't expect school to be easy: They expect it to be accessible. They don't expect special treatment (in fact they often resent it). They expect reasonable accommodation to learning impediments, testing difficulties, and problems with stress or attention deficit. (Mosley, 1994, p. 4)

Learning Disabilities and Psychiatric Disabilities

Often learning disabilities coexist with psychiatric disabilities. Some students request accommodations for learning disabilities as a way of not disclosing their psychiatric disabilities. However, after requesting accommodation for a psychiatric disability, students often discover that they have a learning disability. This is particularly true for older students who were in elementary and secondary school before screening for learning disabilities was standard practice. Some of the common problems these disabilities share are

- Difficulty in screening out environmental stimuli
- Problems managing time and deadlines
- Limited ability to tolerate noise and crowds
- Difficulty focusing on multiple tasks simultaneously
- Extreme reactions to negative feedback
- Noticeable anxiety and confusion when given verbal instructions
- Limited ability to tolerate interruptions
- Difficulty switching modalities (e.g., from listening to writing) (Fredo, 1993)

The process for determining accommodations for either disability is similar, but with the discovery of learning disabilities, students may find that new learning strategies or accommodations assist them with problems they had attributed to their psychiatric disability.

SETTING GOALS

What are realistic educational goals for students with a history of a mental disorder? The answer to that question is the same as for any student. Things to consider in assessing potential outcomes are education history and grades, abilities and aptitudes, work history, study skills, motivation, and personal circumstances. Although some students are referred to college by their mental health workers as a substitute for day treatment, most students return to school on their own and are very serious about their education. In a 1993 study by Unger that involved four sites around the country and 93 participants, students were asked to specify their goals in terms of postsecondary ambitions and personal and career achievement. Results are listed in Table 5.1.

Table 5.1. Goals for postsecondary education and personal and career achievements

Goal	Number	Percentage
Associate degree	24	26.7
Four-year degree	21	22.3
Vocational/technical certificate	15	16.0
Transfer to another college	15	16.0
Personal development	14	14.9
New career or skill	12	12.8
Maintain certificate/license	9	13.6
A.A./A.S. Vocational tech major	7	7.4
Improve job skills	6	6.4
Activities courses	0	0.0
Undecided	22	23.4

Note: These items are not mutually exclusive. Participants could have chosen one or more goals. The figures listed in the "Number" column therefore exceed the total number of individuals studied.

A.A., Associate in Arts; A.S., Associate in Science.

Students may need academic advisement to help them set goals that reflect their interests, abilities, and aptitudes. A thorough exploration process will improve motivation and success as they begin their academic work. The outcome of this exploration should be an individualized education program (IEP) that states the educational goals, the steps to achieve the goal, and the accommodations necessary for pursuing the goal. (See Chapter 7 for an example of an IEP.)

SKILLS FOR DISABILITY STUDENT SERVICE COUNSELORS

Many DS counselors feel ill equipped to work with students with psychiatric disabilities because of the student's history of mental illness. This may be a new field of disabilities for which their training had not prepared them. However, the same interpersonal and counseling skills apply. Active listening, clarifying, and paraphrasing skills are needed as well as the attributes of warmth, empathy, and respect. Knowledge about identifying and gaining access to community resources and the ability to advocate are needed. Academic counseling and knowledge of campus resources are the same as those provided for students with other disabilities. The primary difference between students with psychiatric disabilities and those with other disabilities is that the students with the psychiatric disabilities may need more support initially. As they get acclimated to the campus and to the routine of academic work, the need for support is usually reduced.

Some counselors find it helpful to be able to consult with a mental health professional if they are unsure about how to help a student or how to understand the student's symptoms and/or disability. Training in crisis intervention also may give a greater sense of mastery and control. Typically, as counselors become more accustomed to working with this new group of students, they become more comfortable in their role.

Operating Values

In order to work successfully with students with psychiatric disabilities, college staff must hold certain values. The values are based on the following fundamental beliefs about students with psychiatric disabilities:

- People with psychiatric disabilities have a right to be in school and to use the resources of that institution.
- People with psychiatric disabilities come to school with the intent to have a productive and successful educational experience.
- People with psychiatric disabilities can learn and be successful in an academic setting.
- People with psychiatric disabilities are responsible and productive members of the community.
- People with psychiatric disabilities have a right to self-determination and to set their own goals and timelines within the policies of the institution.
- People with psychiatric disabilities have a right to learn from their mistakes and to have the opportunity to grow over time.

Academic Counseling

Students with a history of a mental illness are often out of school for some time before they return to resume their academic instruction. They may have previously attempted to return to school but were unsuccessful because they lacked the necessary support. Their anxiety and fear of failure needs to be taken into account as the process of academic counseling begins. The development of an IEP gives the process of academic counseling a structure and process. It will take away some of the uncertainty of being on campus. The development of the plan may take several semesters as the student adjusts to his or her new role.

Role Clarification

It is important that DS counselors themselves are very clear about their roles. They also may need to remind students and other college staff about the parameters of their roles. They are not clinical therapists and should not function as such. If a mental health problem is identified or if the nature of the problem is uncertain, a mental health provider, either at the school or in the community, should be consulted. DS counselors should limit their roles to providing accommodations, academic counseling, advocacy, and referral. They are not responsible for therapeutic counseling or medication maintenance. If they become too involved with the students' mental health issues or move beyond their prescribed roles, they may become frustrated, disheartened, and reluctant to work with students with mental illness.

Just as they are not therapists, neither are DS counselors disciplinarians. Often, when a student with a behavior problem is identified and there is suspicion that his or her behavior is unusual, the student is referred to the DS office. Although the student may benefit from services and may choose to be identified as having a disability at the time, it is not the counselor's role to confront the student about his or her behavior. This is the role of the staff person who oversees violations of the student code of conduct. If the DS counselor has the student on his or her caseload, the counselor may be able to help the student to explore why his or her behavior became problematic; but neither discipline nor classroom management in absentia is the DS counselor's role.

Questions to Guide Practice

Based on the preceding information, the following questions may help the DS counselor stay on track when he or she is working with students with psychiatric disabilities:

1. *How would I solve this problem if the person had a physical disability?* Step back from the psychiatric disability. Consider the person as a student with a problem and proceed accordingly.
2. *What reasonable accommodations need to be made?* If there is a problem in learning or behavior, ask the student whether there is an accommodation that will ameliorate the problem. Often difficult problems can be solved if the underlying cause is understood.
3. *Is this an educational problem or a treatment problem?* This question relates to the DS counselor's role and clarifies whether the difficulty is academic or psychiatric. If the difficulty is psychiatric, a referral should be made.
4. *Do I need to make a referral to a community or campus resource?* This is another question related to the DS counselor's role. Because counselors cannot be all things to all people, other resources may be needed. The question is whether the resource is available on or off campus.

5. *Has there been a violation of the student code of conduct?* If the student
    has violated the code of conduct, then it is a problem that other col-
    lege staff should be made aware of and be involved in.
6. *Am I working harder on this problem than the student who presented the
    problem?* Sometimes counselors get very invested in the outcomes
    for a particular student. They take on tasks that the students should
    do themselves. It may seem easier to make the telephone call or to
    see the instructor for the student rather than have the student do it,
    but such an action may be a disservice to all (Unger, 1991).

Making Referrals

It is helpful if DS counselors know the community resources needed by
students with psychiatric disabilities so they can make a referral. Handbooks of human services resources published by mental health advocates, consumers or professionals, mental health associations, the National Alliance for the Mentally Ill, mental health clinics, county or state
mental health divisions, community libraries, and telephone books are
all important sources of information. There are many national organizations that are also good sources of information. (See the Appendix at
the end of this book for a list of several of these organizations.)

The decision about whether to make a referral should be made
jointly by the student and the counselor. The person or resource to
whom the student is referred should reflect the student's needs and
values. For example, a student may need to have a case manager to
help him or her obtain housing or Social Security benefits. The student
may prefer working with one agency over another, with a male rather
than a female, with someone who is older than he or she is, or with
someone who is located close to his or her home. If a provider can be
found who matches the student's needs, the probability of success of
the referral and the work that needs to be done is maximized.

Davidson (1993) made the following suggestions for helping the
student to identify and contact the resource he or she needs:

1. Listen to the student carefully. Encourage him or her to tell the
    whole story. When the student is finished, summarize to be sure
    that you understand everything.
2. Once a story is clear, ask the student what he or she wants done.
    Some students may just want to talk.
3. If help is to be given in contacting a resource, be certain that the
    student has given permission to do so and keep him or her in-
    formed of each step taken.

4. Do not do more than is requested. Support the student's decisions and provide information.
5. Recognize the limitations of the counselor's role. Do not promise to do something and then fail to do it.
6. Allow the student to play an active role in clarifying the problem, finding an advocate, or seeking information.
7. A student's frustration may be the result of an inability to communicate in an effective manner. Teach the student how to be polite but firm.

The more students can take responsibility for themselves, the more independent they can become. Although they may initially require more DS assistance, they will require less personal time as they gain confidence and knowledge about going to school.

PROGRAM MODELS

Some colleges have developed programs to address issues raised by having students with psychiatric disabilities on their campuses. These programs, or in some cases committees, have developed strategies that work on their campuses with their particular resources and needs. Several program models are presented in the next section to provide ideas of how others have worked together to solve problems.

Individualized Accommodation Planning Team

The Office for Campus Access at the University of Arkansas recognized that many students with psychiatric disabilities who were enrolled at their school had difficulty staying in school (Serebrenni & Waitzman, 1995). This difficulty in maintaining enrollment often stemmed from inadequate support. The office also recognized that education plays an important role for students in enhancing recovery and reintegrating them into their communities. To assist the students to remain in school, the university developed a group of services, collectively called the Individualized Accommodation Planning Team, to consolidate and expand the support given.

The Individualized Accommodation Planning Team includes a licensed examiner, the student's academic advisor, graduate students from the clinical psychology doctoral program who act as case managers, consultants from the psychology department, and the student's therapist (if appropriate). The services include academic accommodations, case managers to monitor student progress, and a class that students with psychiatric disabilities are encouraged to attend.

The accommodations that are provided generally include extended time for exams, test-taking in a nondistracting environment, notetaking assistance, tape-recording lectures, and extensions on projects/exams if the student's disability prevents him or her from meeting deadlines. Case managers are involved in the intake process, assessment, and the provision of accommodations. They also provide support to the students. The class assists students with psychiatric disabilities or other hidden disabilities with communication skills, self-advocacy, stress management, increasing self-esteem, and time management.

The University of Arkansas has made a commitment to helping students with psychiatric disabilities stay in school. By rethinking how it delivers services and who should be involved in the delivery of those services, it has developed a team that solves problems for the university and for its students.

Mentoring as a Support Service

The University of Virginia has developed a mentoring program to assist students with psychiatric disabilities to stay in school and learn how to be more successful in the academic environment (Brown, 1994). At the heart of the program is the relationship developed between the mentor and the student. The mentor and the student work together to clarify the student's values and goals and to develop time management skills. The time management skills are seen as essential to help students examine and organize all facets of their lives. The relationship provides support to the student and a safe environment in which to practice new skills.

Staff mentoring pairs a disability support staff member with a student diagnosed with a psychological disability. Expertise in the treatment of mental disorders is not a necessity; rather, the mentor should be familiar with the student's disability and its manifestations. The meetings between the two become a time for the student to get support and to discuss issues related to all facets of his or her life. As a result of the meaningful relationship established, students sometimes bring increasingly complex issues to their mentors. The program has developed an interdisciplinary approach so other professionals involved with the student can also be consulted to assist with problems.

Mentoring is an adjunct to other accommodations. It is designed to help students stay in school and to solve problems as they arise. It gives the student personal support, which can often mean the difference between success and failure.

Diabasis: The Bridge to Coordinated Services for Students at Risk   *Diabasis* is defined as the bridge between two bases; it is also the name of the student mental health services committee at the College of the Redwoods. The college is located in Northern California in a rural setting and, prior to Diabasis, did not have a student mental health services staff or any crisis intervention personnel (Parton, Amada, & Unger, 1991). There were few mental health services available in the community. In order to coordinate services to students who needed additional help, staff from many departments of the college held periodic meetings to solve various problems. Members of the informal committee included staff from counseling, DS, learning disabilities programs, the dormitories, campus security, career center, financial aid, the dean of student services, and faculty (as required).

The problems Diabasis addressed included students who were disruptive; students who had problems in academic, social, psychological, or financial areas; or students who used a number of campus services, causing confusion and frustration for the students themselves and the staff. The purpose was to determine the scope of the college's ability to assist the student and to make recommendations and referrals. The goal was to help the student succeed on campus.

The Diabasis committee developed an educational case manager system in which Diabasis members monitor and work with students who are at risk for mental illness. The committee developed an effective follow-up system, learned about the community resources so it could make appropriate referrals as an alternative to school, developed better administrative supports, and provided in-service training for all staff. The success of the program is attributed to the role clarification that comes from the interdisciplinary teamwork.

The Student Mental Health Committee   Rancho Santiago College is located in an urban/suburban setting in Southern California (Parton, Amada, & Unger, 1991). The dean of students designated an interdisciplinary interagency team, known as the Student Mental Health Committee, to be a permanent campus committee. The purpose of the collaborative effort among on- and off-campus professionals is to identify and manage students at risk and provide a rapid response to student problems. It also provides follow up with referrals to on- and off-campus services. The goal is to help students at risk succeed.

Members of the Student Mental Health Committee include the dean of students (chair), DS counselors, a psychologist, an Employment Center counselor, an academic counselor, a faculty member, a continuing education counselor, the coordinator of student health, the county mental health administrator, the director of county mental health outpatient services, staff from county social services agencies, and staff from the Department of Vocational Rehabilitation.

The committee identifies students at risk, develops a volunteer crisis team, assigns each student with a volunteer case manager, provides campus members with information on community resources and how to utilize them, provides staff development, and presents information about the program to political and funding entities.

SUMMARY

Students with mental disorders are returning to school in increasing numbers. As DS counselors work with these individuals, the stigma seems to fall away, and they become similar to any other student who needs special services. Some students require more services than others; some are brighter or more adaptable. Sometimes, as with all students, there are difficult ones. The important thing is to work with and provide services to this group of students as you would provide services to any other group.

REFERENCES

American Psychiatric Association. (1994). *Diagnostic and statistical manual of mental disorders* (4th ed.). Washington, DC: Author.

Americans with Disabilities Act (ADA) of 1990, PL 101-336, 42 U.S.C. §§ 12101 *et seq.*

Brown, R. (1994, Fall). Mentoring as an adjunct accommodation for students with psychological disabilities (PD Newsletter). In *Psychological disabilities: A collection of readings prepared for the 1996 AHEAD TRIO Training Program* (pp. 14–15). Columbus, OH: Association on Higher Education and Disability.

Cavendor, L. (1994, Winter). Skills critical for students and staff. In *Psychological disabilities: A collection of readings prepared for the 1996 AHEAD TRIO Training Program* (pp. 11–12). Columbus, OH: Association on Higher Education and Disability.

Davidson, H. (1993). *Just ask: A handbook for instructors of students with mental disorders.* Calgary, Alberta, Canada: Detselig Enterprises, Ltd.

Dougherty, S., Kampana, K., Kontos, R., Flores, M., Lockhart, R., & Shaw, D. (1996). Supported education: A qualitative study of the student experience. *Psychiatric Rehabilitation Journal, 19*(3), 59–70.

Fredo, L. (1993). *Learning diversity: Accommodations in colleges and universities for students with mental illness.* Toronto, Ontario, Canada: Canadian Mental Health Association.

HEATH Resource Center and Association on Higher Education and Disability. (n.d.). *Americans with Disabilities Act.* Washington DC, Columbus, OH: Author.

Hoffmann F., & Mastrianni, X. (1989). The mentally ill student on campus: Theory and practice. *Journal of American College Health, 38,* 15–22.

Jarrow, J. (n.d.). *Subpart E: The impact of Section 504 on postsecondary education.* Columbus, OH: Association on Higher Education and Disability.

Mosley, L.E. (1994, September). *Education and persons with a psychiatric disability.* Paper presented at the Therapeutic Education Conference, San Diego, CA.

Parton, D. (1993). Implementation of a systems approach to supported education at four community college model service sites. *Psychosocial Rehabilitation Journal, 17*(1), 171–188.

Parton, D., Amada G., & Unger, K. (1991). *Resource guide for serving students with psychological disabilities in the California Community Colleges.* Sacramento: California Community Colleges Chancellor's Office, Disabled Student Programs and Services.

Rehabilitation Act of 1973, PL 93-112, 29 U.S.C. §§ 701 *et seq.*

Serebrenni, R., & Waitzman, B. (1995, Spring). Accommodations for students with psychiatric disabilities at the University of Arkansas, Office for Campus Access. In *Psychological disabilities: A collection of readings prepared for the 1996 AHEAD TRIO Training Program* (p. 14). Columbus, OH: Association on Higher Education and Disability.

Unger, K. (1991). Serving students with psychiatric disabilities on campus: Clarifying the disabled student services counselor's role. *Journal of Post-Secondary Education and Disability, 9*(4), 278–281.

Unger, K. (1993). Creating supported education programs utilizing existing community resources. *Psychosocial Rehabilitation Journal, 17*(1), 11–23.

Unger, K. (1996). *Annual performance report to NIDRR on supplemental education project.* Tucson: University of Arizona.

Unger, K. (1997). *Annual performance report to NIDRR on supplemental education project.* Tucson: University of Arizona.

Wilson, M. (1995, Winter). Dual diagnosis of psychological and learning disabilities: The role of psychotropic medication in assessment and treatment of learning disabilities (PD Newsletter). In *Psychological Disabilities: A collection of readings prepared for the 1996 AHEAD TRIO Training Program* (pp. 8–9). Columbus: OH: Association on Higher Education and Disability.

6

Health and Safety
Issues on Campus

Classroom instructors may fear the possibility of violent disrup-
tion [by their students with psychiatric disabilities], but will more
often encounter difficulties of another kind: persons who are overly
talkative, labile, easily threatened, highly anxious, dependent or
a host of other idiosyncratic expressions of the person's illness
or their fear of failure. These instructors will require training and
support in learning ways of testing, of issuing assignments, of
conducting classroom discussions and of setting appropriate
boundaries which are respectful of the individual and to the disci-
pline they are teaching. (Mosley, 1994, p. 4)

Mostly, we would like the world to see us as able to recover, able to
make a contribution, able to be in every degree human and worth
being seen as individuals with separate aspirations, gifts, degrees
of taste, and desires to learn. We have become rather weary of being
the last odd lot of society's unwanted. (Mosley, 1994, p. 1)

One of the fears of some disability services (DS) counselors is that
students with psychiatric disabilities will be disruptive on campus or
threaten the health and safety of staff and other students. Although

101

some students with psychiatric disabilities may be disruptive, they are not, as a rule, more disruptive than other students (Parton, 1993). It is important, however, that, should an incident occur, DS staff and counselors have the information and skills they need to deal with the situation safely and effectively.

The California Community College System Chancellor's Office Report defined a *student who is disruptive* as one who

> Verbally threatens or abuses college personnel, physically threatens or assaults others, willfully damages college property, misuses drugs or alcohol on college premises, habitually interferes with the learning environment by disruptive verbal or behavioral expressions, or persistently makes inordinate demands for time and attention from faculty and staff. (Parton, Amada, & Unger, 1991, p. 72)

Most students with a psychiatric disability will attend school, complete their coursework without drawing inordinate amounts of attention to themselves, and move on. Others, perhaps because they may not be stable enough to be on campus, or they may become ill because of medication or life changes on campus, may exhibit signs of distress or psychiatric symptoms and be disruptive. Others may be extremely vulnerable to the demands and stresses of the college campus and exhibit disruptive behavior in difficult situations. A fourth category of disruptive students includes those individuals who have a history of behavior problems in a school setting, abuse drugs or alcohol, or have a history of violent behavior. It is helpful to understand the cause of the student's behavior so that intervention is appropriate.

SUPPORTING POSITIVE BEHAVIOR

The first step in supporting positive behavior is to provide the necessary services of academic advising and accommodations. A good working relationship between the student and his or her DS counselor may prevent disruptive or nonproductive behavior. Good classroom management skills may avert an incident. It is also important to understand why student behavior becomes problematic. Some students behave inappropriately because of changes in medication or difficulty managing increased stress, or perhaps they are on the verge of a relapse. Others may have difficulty managing their symptoms. An observant staff person may often intervene by referring the student to a counselor or by providing additional support.

When an incident does occur, it is critical that the proper policies be in place to meet the needs of all students, including those with psychiatric disabilities. The following administrative supports are needed:

- A clear, behavioral definition of disruptive behavior
- A well-defined code of student conduct
- Judicial affairs policies and procedures
- Designated administrative personnel responsible for implementation
- A feedback mechanism for monitoring outcomes (Pavela, 1985)

A student code of conduct and supporting policies provide the structure for consistent and methodical interventions. They are tools that protect the rights of both students and the staff.

Do college staff have a role in preventing disruptive behavior? Although it is up to the student to manage his or her own behavior, experienced staff know that providing support services may, in actuality, be preventive. Providing good academic planning and counseling, identifying potential problems and functional limitations, identifying previous experiences in school, and providing accommodations will help to decrease stress and frustration and, thus, help prevent inappropriate behavior. Forging a close relationship with the student also allows the DS counselor an opportunity to see changes in the student over time. If the changes are remarkable, it may be appropriate to make a referral to a mental health provider.

Other staff also have a role in supporting positive student behavior. Good classroom management with clearly defined rules for behavior helps to set clear expectations. Timely interventions prevent a situation from escalating and give the student the opportunity to learn from his or her behavior. Timely interventions also help to ameliorate frustration on the part of both student and staff. Monitoring behavior on campus through administrative policies and procedures also provides continued guidance to students about appropriate behavior.

CLASSROOM MANAGEMENT STRATEGIES

In a classroom setting, both students and instructors have rights and responsibilities. Any classroom management strategy should be based on these mutually shared rights and responsibilities. Although it is not the DS counselor's role to provide this kind of training to instructors, they may provide guidance to instructors to help them to work more effectively with students who pose problems in the classroom. The basic principles discussed in the subsections that follow may be helpful in providing a base on which to develop classroom policies and procedures.

Principles of Classroom Management

Instructors are responsible for maintaining a good learning environment in their classrooms that is respectful of the students, the learning process, and the instructors themselves. Principles for classroom management for instructors include the following:

- Each person has the right to be treated with respect and positive regard.
- Each person has the ability to learn and the right to an education.
- Each person has the right to express him- or herself in a manner that reflects his or her individual personality, values, and culture. (It is important to remember that this expression should not interfere with the primary functions of the classroom.)
- It is the instructor's responsibility to provide the educational leadership and primary instruction in the classroom in such a manner that meets the learning needs of the students.
- It is the instructor's responsibility to set the behavior standards in the classroom, which are based on the institution's code of student conduct, and to enforce conduct in the manner specified by the code.

Guidelines for Classroom Behavior

Students should manage their own behavior in the classroom, but they may need some reminders from the instructor that their behavior affects the learning of others. Disruptive behavior is often triggered by emotional turmoil. When this occurs, the instructor should not avoid the situation but address it directly, with a minimum of intervention needed to calm the situation. Sometimes instructors are reluctant to impose disciplinary procedures on students with psychiatric disabilities. This is a disservice to both the student and staff. Timely interventions prevent the situation from getting worse and give the student the opportunity to learn from his or her behavior. Supplying each student with a set of general guidelines at the beginning of each term helps to make expectations concrete. Guidelines for classroom behavior for students include the following:

1. Students should complete all assignments on schedule, unless other arrangements have been made.
2. Students should arrive and be seated so that class can start on time.
3. Students should be prepared to participate in class discussions in a meaningful way and in a manner that enhances their own and others' learning.
4. Students should conduct themselves in such a manner that their behavior does not hamper the instructor in teaching the class or take away from the learning experience of others.

Guidelines for the Instructor

When a student is being disruptive, it is important that the instructor let the student know that he or she is aware of the student's behavior. Because the instructor's primary task is teaching, he or she should not interrupt the class any more than necessary. A classroom management strategy that calls for a minimum amount of intervention is described in the next sections, but it is important to remember that involvement should increase if the student does not respond with changes in his or her behavior. The following are guidelines for the instructor in maintaining a positive learning environment.

Observe   Watch the student to see if the behavior will stop momentarily. If it does not stop, catch the student's eye so he or she understands that he or she is being watched.

Engage   If the behavior continues, address the student directly (by name or at his or her desk or chair if possible) in order to detract as little as possible from classroom activities. Get more information. Ask the student if he or she has a question or if there is a problem that needs attention. If the issue cannot be resolved at the time, make an appointment to see the student after class.

Intervene   If the behavior does not stop, ask the student to step outside for a brief conference. Put someone else in charge of the class for the interim. If this is a crisis situation, dismiss the class. Get more information from the student to determine whether he or she has a particular problem or concern about something. Keep the discussion focused in the present moment and on the student's behavior. Next, ask the student to stop the behavior. If the student does not feel he or she can stop the behavior, ask the student to leave the class for now, and set up an appointment with him or her before the next class to resolve the issue.

In the meeting, explore the student's problem further to determine whether an accommodation or a referral is necessary. If neither are the case and there are no another issues, determine whether the student is willfully and intentionally disruptive. If so, explain the process for managing disruptive students outlined in the student code of conduct.

Consult   If a meeting does not resolve the problem and the behavior continues, begin the process of involving other staff members. Notify the dean of students. Talk with other college staff to determine whether the student has a problem in other classes or other places on campus. Talk to the student's advisor. If possible, set up a case conference. Decide whether it is necessary to begin a formal process. Inform the student of the process being implemented. Instructors are often reluctant to involve others in a problem they feel it is their job to handle. However, there may be several other people that are struggling with the same student and the same behavior. It is in the student's best interest to have the problem identified and resolved before it escalates into a major issue.

Document   It is important to keep records of what has been done to solve the problem. Records provide a means to monitor the situation and to determine whether it has improved; they also provide a basis for any formal action that might take place.

Instructors should not hesitate to resolve problems early. They are often powerful change agents. Compassionate understanding and firm guidelines may be a positive force in the student's life at that moment.

Crisis Intervention

If a crisis (i.e., when a student becomes very agitated, aggressive, or threatens the health and safety of him- or herself or others) occurs, the situation requires immediate and specific attention. The following guidelines for managing a crisis are recommended for all college staff and instructors (Cavendor, 1996):

Remain calm. Take a deep breath and relax. A calm demeanor will have a soothing impact on the student. A calm persona will help keep the situation in control and reassure the student.

Listen to the student. Allow the student to talk about what has happened and vent his or her feelings. Respond to the student's feelings with empathy and respect. Avoid confrontational behavior.

Focus the student. Help the student to focus on the here and now.

Ask for direction. Is there something that the student wants done or that he or she wants to do by him- or herself? What would the student like you to do?

Refer the student to help. Before leaving the student, make sure that he or she is calm and in control. If there are any questions about the student being in control, do not leave him or her. Call campus security or 911 for assistance or walk the student to a mental health office or DS office and make sure he or she is seen by somebody who is skilled in handling such situations.

Working with
Students with Behavior Problems

Similar to all other students, each student with psychiatric disabilities is an individual. The student's behavior and how his or her symptoms are manifested are unique. However, the experiences of college staff have led them to identify patterns of behavior that run across the entire student body—including those with psychiatric difficulties—and that require specific notice and interventions.

Canada College (Redwood City, California), Portland Community College (Portland, Oregon), and DeAnza College (Cupertino, California) recommended the following additional hints for DS counselors and instructors for managing particular types of student behavior.

1. The Student Who Is Verbally Aggressive A student may become verbally aggressive when he or she feels frustrated or out of control. He or she will lash out at others as a way to express these feelings. *Do* allow the student to vent and describe what is upsetting him or her but indicate that verbally abusive behavior is not acceptable. If the student gets too close to you, sit down and ask him or her to move back. Be aware of the closest exit. If necessary, walk the student to a quieter, but public place; if the student agrees, walk him or her to the counselor's office or to Campus Security. *Do not* enlist the aid of other students to quiet the student down. *Do not* threaten, taunt, or push the student. *Do not* press for an explanation of the student's behavior. *Do not* get physically cornered.

2. The Student Who Is Violent or Physically Destructive A student may become violent when he or she feels totally frustrated and unable to do anything about it. Being frustrated over a long period of time may erode the student's control over his or her behavior. This behavior may present the most immediate danger to staff and to other students. *Do* get help immediately from Campus Security or the counseling or DS office. *Do* present a calm appearance and let the student talk. Respond to him or her calmly and quietly. Explain that only behaviors that are safe for others are acceptable. Call for assistance, but first tell the student of your intention. *Do not* threaten, taunt, or push the student. *Do not* press for an explanation of the student's behavior. *Do not* confront or threaten the student. *Do not* get physically cornered.

3. The Student Who Is in Poor Contact with Reality A student in poor contact with reality may be having hallucinations or delusions or have difficulty separating fact from fantasy. He or she may behave in strange or unusual ways and is most likely scared, frightened, and overwhelmed; he or she probably is not dangerous. *Do* respond to the student with care and kindness, and maintain eye contact. Acknowledge the student's fears without either supporting or contradicting his or her misconceptions. Try to change the focus from the student's delusion to the immediate reality. Contact the counseling or DS office. *Do not* argue or try to convince the student that he or she is irrational. *Do not* play along with the student's delusions. *Do* *not* demand, command, or order the student. *Do not* expect customary responses.

4. The Student Who Is Depressed A student who is depressed may go unnoticed. His or her behavior may indicate low energy, lack of interest in what is going on around him or her, feelings of sadness and hopelessness, and difficulties with eating and sleeping. His or her personal hygiene may be poor. *Do* express concern and privately inquire if he or she is receiving any help. If not, make a referral or escort the student to the counseling or DS office. *Do not* discount the significance and intensity of the student's feelings. *Do not* say things such as, "Crying won't help." *Do not* discount a suicide threat. If the student says he or she is contemplating suicide, notify the counseling or DS office, and give the student a crisis hotline number in his or her community. *Do not* leave the student unattended unless he or she has agreed to a positive course of action, such as calling a hotline or seeing a mental health services provider.

5. The Student Who Is Anxious A student who is anxious appears overly concerned with trivial matters. He or she may require very specific guidelines and seek more structure in assignments. Unfamiliar or new situations often raise his or her anxiety. Apprehension over assignments and concerns about perfection may be a result of unreasonably high self-expectations. *Do* be clear and explicit about expectations. Let the student express his or her feeling and thoughts. Recommend that he or she seek counseling or DS assistance. Remain patient with the student's demands for clarification and structure. *Do not* discount the student's anxiety by saying, "It's not really that bad, is it?" *Do not* blame yourself for the student's anxiety.

6. The Student Who Is Dependent A student who is dependent may attach him- or herself to staff and demand more and more time. He or she is often lonely and has poor interpersonal skills. The student may see the amount of attention given to him- or herself as a reflection of his or her self-worth. *Do* set limits on the time spent with the student and limits on which subjects will be discussed. *Do* let the student make his or her own decisions. Refer the student for counseling. *Do not* let the student use staff as his or her only source of support. *Do not* assume the role of parental figure, give advice, or give more time and energy than can be realistically spent or is appropriate.

7. The Student Who Is Suspicious A student who is suspicious often is tense and distrustful. He or she may interpret minor oversights as personal rejection and overreact to insignificant occurrences. He or she is overly concerned with fairness and being treated equally. The student may place staff in seemingly no-win situations because he or she views attention as the staff wanting something from him or her and inattention as the staff having it in for him or her. *Do* express compassion without overstating friendship. Suspicious students often have trouble relating to others. *Do* be firm, steady, punctual, and consistent. Be specific and clear regarding the standards of behavior expected from the student. *Do* make a referral to counseling. *Do not* become the student's friend. *Do not* be overly warm and nurturing. *Do not* be cute or humorous; this can be misinterpreted as slights or rejections. *Do not* challenge or agree with any misconception.

8. The Student Who Is Seductive A student who is seductive may behave flirtatiously, ask many personal questions, make demands on staff time, and request special treatment. The student may misinterpret attention as meaning staff have special feelings for him or her. *Do* set limits on the amount of time spent with the student and which subjects will be discussed. See the student only in a classroom or an office. Keep the door open during meetings. Be careful about giving double messages or saying things that might be misinterpreted as having a personal interest in the student beyond the normal student–teacher relationship. *Do not* encourage the student by responding positively to inappropriate behavior. *Do not* give the student special treatment.

9. The Student Who Talks About Suicide The student who talks about suicide may mention in an offhand way that he or she wants to kill him- or herself or that he or she thinks about being dead or in a better place. The student may feel depressed and hopeless. He or she may threaten to do something that will end his or her life. *Do* take these threats or comments seriously. If the student mentions specifics about how or when he or she will kill him- or herself or if he or she has made a previous attempt, consider the risk very serious and get help. Express your concern for the student and strongly encourage him or her to see a counselor immediately. Escort the student to the counselor or to someone who can facilitate an appropriate referral. *Do not* make light of suicide threats. *Do not* discount the significance of the student's feelings of depression and hopelessness.

Working with Students with a Borderline Personality Disorder

Some DS providers find working with students who have been diagnosed as having a borderline personality disorder particularly difficult. Although the students can be demanding and somewhat unpredictable in their requests for services, they also can be very bright and engaging as students. Sometimes their behavior angers and frustrates providers, and, as a result, they are often described as being manipulative, exaggerating symptoms, and resisting treatment.

It is important to remember that a borderline personality disorder diagnosis, by definition, is a "pervasive pattern of instability of interpersonal relationships, self-image, and affects, and marked impulsivity" (American Psychiatric Association, 1994, p. 650). It occurs when personality traits become inflexible and maladaptive, causing great distress and functional impairment. (See Chapter 3 for a more detailed discussion of personality disorders.)

Valcov (1994) expanded on the clinical diagnosis by explaining that there are serious problems in three interrelated areas of personality organization and functioning:

1. *Handling affect:* There is a problem in managing overwhelming, raw emotions, especially rage that is experienced as an uncontrollable, alien force from within and threatens to destroy everything. Efforts to control the feelings by shutting down or silent suffering lead to the buildup of tension and the eventual, explosive acting out of impulses and feelings.
2. *Sense of self:* There is a terrible fear of losing oneself and being destroyed. Self-inflicted pain and suicide attempts often bring a release of tension. The experience of inflicting pain tends to bring the self back together and results in getting help and reestablishing contact with others.
3. *Relationships:* There is a great need for contact and support from others coupled with a very basic distrust and fear of being controlled, abandoned, or abused. People may be divided into categories of "good" and "bad," and it is not possible for the person with the diagnosis to integrate both of those characteristics in another person or him- or herself. Someone who may have been helpful initially may disappoint and then become "bad," so the student will go on to someone else. This is the "splitting" that occurs when one person seems to be played against another.

Working with a person with a borderline personality disorder can be challenging because of the characteristics of the disorder. Complying with the following guidelines may help the relationship be mutually satisfactory:

- Be clear, direct, and consistent in all communications.
- Be kind and helpful but not personal and overly friendly.
- Define what is appropriate behavior.
- Define the counselor's role clearly (i.e., what can and cannot be done).
- Document plans so that expectations are clear and mutual.
- Consult with colleagues often if coordination is necessary.

- Get support or consult with a mental health professional.
- Watch for extreme personal reactions (i.e., being overly involved or overly frustrated).

Valcov said the following:

> As a practicing psychotherapist, my clients with borderline personality disorder are among my most challenging cases but are also among the most intelligent and courageous people I know. They are some of the people from whom I learn the most about the human condition and I am deeply grateful for their willingness to share with me their inner experiences. (1994, p. 8)

An excellent clinical resource for working with students with this diagnosis is *Cognitive-Behavioral Treatment of Borderline Personality Disorder* (Lineham, 1993a) and its companion book, *Skills Training for Treating Borderline Personality Disorder* (Lineham, 1993b).

Putting Strategies into Practice

Although the categories of students described in the previous section may relate to dealing with particular symptoms of mental illness, the strategies will be helpful support for many different kinds of students. For example, someone who is using drugs or alcohol may be verbally aggressive or physically violent. A student who is homesick may be depressed and dependent.

Many instructors have become resentful of the additional demands placed on them for managing student behavior and providing accommodations. Each demand takes additional time away from the traditional tasks of teaching, instructional preparation, and student advising. Instructors are required to be not only an experts in their fields but also managers. DS counselors also find their roles and responsibilities expanding. With the increasing diversity of the students who attend college and the increased opportunity and demand for a college education, the classroom makeup and student needs are no longer homogeneous. However, postsecondary education for more people will most certainly mean a higher standard of living and a better quality of life for all.

ASSESSMENT OF PERCEIVED DANGEROUS SITUATIONS AND COPING STRATEGIES

DS or other education staff generally do not need to be concerned about their health and safety when working with people with mental illness. The education environment does not support aggressive or violent behavior, nor does it generally tolerate drug and alcohol abuse. However, because violence by this group of individuals is a common fear for some education staff, assessment of threatening situations and coping strategies are important (see Table 6.1).

If feelings of uneasiness about the student arise, however slight, meet with the student where there are other people and where you can remove yourself. If you have to have a private meeting with someone, ask that a mental health professional or other qualified person sit in with you. Your first responsibility is to yourself and your own sense of safety.

There are several things that an instructor should not do when dealing with students who may be threatening:

- Do not argue with the student.
- Do not threaten the student.

Table 6.1.   Assessment of dangerous situations and coping strategies

Predicting dangerousness
- Assess the person's sobriety. Has he or she been using drugs or alcohol?
- Has the person stopped using his or her medications?
- Does he or she have a history of violent behavior?
- Is he or she highly agitated or incoherent?

Managing dangerousness
- Trust your own instincts. If you feel unsafe, remove yourself from the situation or get help.
- Be honest with yourself. It is normal to be afraid. It is not wise to try to deal with a situation that you are not trained to handle.
- Violence is often the product of anger and fear. Try not to make it worse. Back off if you are in a power struggle or an argument.
- If you cannot remove yourself or the other person from the situation, remain calm. If you are in danger, it is a good idea to ask the person what he or she would like you to do.
- Don't confirm or challenge delusions or hallucinations. It is appropriate for you to say, "I believe these things are real to you."
- Help the individual to find words to express his or her feelings—angry words, scared words, sad words, hopeless words, etc. Words will help express the feelings safely and to calm the individual.
- Keep the person in the here and now. What can be done now to make the situation better for the person right this minute? Help the person to focus on what can be done now. However, the most important idea is, if you feel unsafe, remove yourself from the situation and get help. Call the campus police or dial 911.

From If you fear violence from a mentally ill family member. (1990). *The Journal of the California Alliance of the Mentally Ill, 2,* 7; adapted by permission.

- Do not try to touch the student.
- Do not minimize the student's feelings with statements like, "It isn't that bad."
- Do not make promises that won't be kept (Portland Community College, 1994–1995).

POLICIES AND PRACTICE

Most postsecondary institutions define their missions fairly broadly. They exist not only to promote academic excellence but also to develop informed and conscientious citizens, to honor diversity, and to promote behavior that will sustain and build community. The institution's conduct becomes a model for its students and faculty. Having policies that acknowledge and respect the special needs of its students provides a demonstrable statement of how things could and should be.

As with any special group of individuals, having students with psychiatric disabilities on campuses poses unique challenges. These students may have special needs that, if accommodated, will result in their being able to fully utilize the educational environment. A college or university should be aware of such needs and develop policies that maximize the student's potential to succeed. One such need comes from the episodic nature of mental illness, which can be exacerbated by stress and other life problems.

Medical Leave Policy

If a student needs to leave campus to be hospitalized or to receive more intensive treatment closer to home, policies should be in place to make that transition from school and back onto campus smooth and efficient. The policies should attempt to minimize the loss of financial resources such as grants, loans or scholarships, medical insurance, and housing, as well as college credits. Special attention should be paid to confidentiality so the stigma that often surrounds a mental illness is minimized.

Most colleges and universities have medical leave policies. These policies should be extended to students who need to withdraw from school as a result of mental illness. The policies may need to be amended to take into account the special nature of a psychiatric illness and its disabilities. For example, someone on campus may need to contact the appropriate service entities to make sure that financial concerns have been settled, immediate losses are minimized, and permanent losses are not incurred. Instructors need to be contacted so that incompletes (rather than failures) can be given if possible. If there is still time to drop classes, refunds need to be given. Other factors related to student life need to be attended to so that students can return to campus with a minimum amount of disruption to their personal lives as well as their academic standing.

Psychiatric Leave Policy

Hoffman, Mastrianni, and Stein (1991) recommended that the following be included in a psychiatric leave policy:

1. Students should remain matriculated at the college without the need to reapply. If a student has to leave because of his or her illness, he or she should be able to return without repeating the application process.
2. Students should receive preregistration material and register in absentia for the semester in which they wish to return. To facilitate their returning to school, students should be mailed preregistration materials and be able to register by mail so their return can go smoothly and without the stress of registration.
3. Students should be able, with the instructor's permission, to complete work in absentia or receive "incompletes" to complete coursework upon return or to withdraw from courses without penalty. Students who have to take a psychiatric leave should not be penalized for doing so. They should have the opportunity to complete their coursework in a manner that is agreeable to both the instructor and the student.
4. Students should be eligible for tuition and fee refunds according to the published refund policy. There should be no changes in general refund policy for students who take a psychiatric leave.
5. Students should provide proper documentation from professionals on readiness to return and develop a plan, upon returning, with the college for on- and off-campus supports. To demonstrate the appropriateness of their return to campus, students should develop a clear plan that addresses their medical and support needs so they can complete their coursework successfully.

Guidelines for Disciplinary Withdrawal

Students may sometimes need to withdraw from school because their behavior disrupts the learning environment or because they are a danger to themselves or others. In such a case, a withdrawal may be the appropriate course of action. Pavela suggested that the educational institution do the following to safeguard the student's rights to due process:

- Develop a clear statement of policy for disciplinary withdrawals.
- Provide verification that the student engaged in or threatened to engage in disruptive behavior.
- Provide advance notice to the student that he or she may be subject to a withdrawal.
- Allow the student to examine the evidence against him or her prior to a formal hearing.
- Provide a statement of reasons for any decision made by the institution (1985, p. 25).

In order to institute a policy for disciplinary withdrawal, a student code of conduct must be in place. This code should clearly describe which behaviors are prohibited and which policies and procedures will be followed if a student violates the code. General categories of student behavior for a disciplinary withdrawal might include the following:

- Causing physical harm or intentionally or recklessly causing apprehension of such harm
- Interfering with typical college-sponsored activities such as studying, teaching, research, administration, or any emergency services
- Destroying or theft of college property
- Possessing or storing of illegal substances, weapons, or explosives
- Forgery, unauthorized alteration, or unauthorized use of college documents as instruments of identification
- Presenting false information to the college
- All forms of academic dishonesty, including cheating, fabrication, facilitating academic dishonesty, and plagiarism
- Unauthorized presence in or use of college premises, facilities, or property
- Failing to comply with the lawful direction of college personnel acting in performance of their duties (Pavela, 1985; Portland Community College, 1994/1995)

Sanctions that may result from a disciplinary withdrawal might include the following:

- *Expulsion:* Permanent separation of the student from the college
- *Suspension:* Separation of the student from the university for a specified period of time
- *Disciplinary probation:* Probation with or without the loss of privileges for a definite period of time. The student may not be able to represent the college or to hold office.

- *Disciplinary reprimand:* The student is warned that further miscon-
  duct may result in more severe disciplinary action
- *Restitution:* The student is required to make payment to the college
  or to other people, groups, or organizations for damages incurred
  as a result of his or her actions.
- *Other sanctions:* Other sanctions may be imposed instead of or in
  addition to those previously specified.

Prior to a withdrawal or an imposition of sanctions, a due process
hearing must be held that clearly states the rights and responsibilities
of each person (including the student) and a description of the step-
by-step process for the hearing process (Pavela, 1980). The due process
hearing should include a clear explanation of readmission procedures
after dismissal; a process for reporting, recording, and maintaining
records; and a student grievance procedure.

A disciplinary withdrawal should be used only when all else has
not worked. It should be used to keep others safe and secure and to
help the offending student learn the consequences of his or her actions.
The same is true for students with a mental illness who willfully vio-
late the student code of conduct. In terms of the importance of sanctions as a learning process, Pavela quoted Justice Powell dissenting in
Goss v. Lopez:

> Education in any meaningful sense includes the inoculation of an under-
> standing in each pupil of the necessity of rules and obedience thereto. This
> understanding is no less important than learning to read and write. One
> who does not comprehend the meaning and necessity of discipline is
> handicapped not merely in his education but throughout his subsequent
> life. In an age when the home and church play a diminishing role in shap-
> ing the character and value judgments of the young a heavier responsibil-
> ity falls upon the schools. When an immature student merits censure for
> his conduct, he is rendered a disservice if appropriate sanctions are not
> applied. (1980, p. 152)

SUMMARY

The academic environment is a place for people with a mental illness
to learn about themselves, learn new skills and knowledge, and regain
a legitimate role in society. It is an opportunity that is guaranteed to
them by law; however, with that right comes the responsibility for their
behavior.

REFERENCES

American Psychiatric Association. (1994). *Diagnostic and statistical manual of
mental disorders* (4th ed.). Washington, DC: Author.

Cavendor, L. (1996, Winter). Skills critical for students and staff. *PD Newsletter.* Columbus, OH: Association on Higher Education and Disability.

Goss v. Lopez, 419 U.S. 565 (1975).

Hoffman F., Mastrianni, X., & Stein J. (1991). *Psychiatric leaves of absence: Guidelines for campus policy and practice.* Saratoga Springs, NY: Four Winds Saratoga.

If you fear violence from a mentally ill family member. (1990). *The Journal of the California Alliance of the Mentally Ill, 2,* 7.

Lineham, M. (1993a). *Cognitive-behavioral treatment of borderline personality disorder.* New York: Guilford Press.

Lineham, M. (1993b). *Skills training manual for treating borderline personality disorder.* New York: Guilford Press.

Mosley, L.E. (1994, September). *Education and persons with a psychiatric disability.* Speech presented at the Therapeutic Education Conference, San Diego, CA.

Parton, D. (1993). Implementation of a systems approach to supported education at four community college model service sites. *Psychosocial Rehabilitation Journal, 17*(1), 171–188.

Parton, D., Amada G., & Unger, K. (1991). *Resource guide for serving students with psychological disabilities in the California Community College System.* Sacramento: California Community Colleges Chancellor's Office, Disabled Student Programs and Services.

Pavela G. (1980). Limiting the "pursuit of perfect justice" on campus: A proposed code of student conduct. *Journal of College and University Law, 6,* 137–160.

Pavela, G. (1985). The dismissal of students with mental disorders. In *The Higher Education Administration Series.* Asheville, NC: College Administration Publications, Inc.

Portland Community College. (1994–1995). *How do I help a student in distress?* Portland, OR: Author

Valcov, A.W. (1994, March). *Borderline personality disorder.* Paper presented at the Wealth of Health Conference, San Mateo, CA.

7

Providing Educational
Services in Mental Health Settings

*I don't know what the big problem is—people need a place to live, a
job, some friends, maybe a chance to go to school, maybe, and learn
something. I don't know what the big problem is. (Anonymous individual with a mental illness, cited in Dougherty, 1997, p. 36)*

*There is not a soul . . . who does not understand what education
means to a person, what it means to the way you feel about yourself, what you come to believe in yourself, what others come to feel
and believe about you—and what you hope for and what others
hope for you. (Dougherty, 1997, p. 36)*

Attending college is an opportunity for individuals with psychiatric
disabilities to apply old skills while learning new ones and regaining a
functional role in society. College is also often the first step to reenter-
ing the labor market. People with a history of mental illness are returning to school in increasing numbers with the hope of developing a
career path rather than working in dead-end or entry-level positions
for the rest of their lives.

In 1991, a service preference survey (Rogers, Walsh, Masotta, &
Danley) conducted with mental health consumers ($N = 314$) in the De-

partment of Mental Health (DMH) in Boston found that 62% of all respondents would like more education. In order to reach their educational goals, between 33% and 52% of the participants wanted supports
such as assistance in applying to an education program, gaining access
to financial aid, and strengthening basic education skills; peer support
groups; or staff support.

Historically, people with a mental illness have been considered to
be incapable of learning and unable to succeed in college. However, an
ongoing supported education study (Unger, 1997) with sites in California, Connecticut, and Massachusetts indicated that students with mental illness ($N = 124$) completed 90% of the classes in which they were enrolled, with a mean grade point average (GPA) of 3.3 on a 4-point scale.

People with mental illnesses who are attending college report a
significantly greater level of satisfaction with their quality of life and
significantly higher levels of self-esteem than those who are working
or who are not enrolled in school and are not working (Unger, 1997).
Thirty-four percent of the students who were enrolled or who had been
enrolled in a supported education program in the previous 6 years were
currently working (Unger, 1997). In addition, a 1991 study (Unger,
Anthony, Sciarappa, & Rogers) reported significantly decreased rates
of hospitalization for these individuals.

An emphasis on postsecondary education services also helps those
who are hospitalized. In a comparison study (Hoffman & Mastrianni,
1993) of two private inpatient psychiatric hospitals that provided services to young adults, the hospital that provided services specifically
designed to help individuals maintain or advance their education goals
found that these individuals were more likely to return to college than
those from the other hospital that did not provide educational support
services (69% versus 47%). These young adults also were significantly
more likely to return as full-time students or to return on a part-time
status and progress to full time (80% versus 58%). In addition, they also
were more likely to maintain their career aspirations (55% versus 37%).

Although people with a history of mental illness want to attend
college, and research has shown that they can do so successfully, there
is a paucity of services available to support their education goals. Mental health programs have not responded with the desired services that
are necessary. There are many reasons for this. The programs may not
be aware that supported education services exist and that they can be
a viable program option. They may not have the resources to fund the
programs. Or, they may not believe that their students with mental illness can benefit from such programs. This chapter addresses these issues and provides guidelines for establishing supported education services in mental health settings.

SUPPORTED EDUCATION PARTICIPANTS

Mental health agencies are designed to serve a variety of individuals with a range of diagnoses and symptoms, as well as levels of severity of illness and disability. The question within this varied group of individuals becomes this: For whom are supported education services most appropriate? Although it is impossible to predict who might be successful in returning to school, several studies have described the mental health participants in their programs (Unger, 1993; Unger et al., 1991).

Unger (1993) attempted to describe a fairly typical supported education participant. The participants in the study ($N = 94$) had a mean age of 35 years and were equally divided between men and women, two thirds were Caucasian, one fourth lived in supported housing, and the majority (69%) received Social Security benefits. Less that half (45%) had been married. More than half (60%) had previously worked an average work week of about 20 hours for an average hourly salary of about $4.79. All of the participants had been diagnosed with a psychiatric illness; 77% had been hospitalized. The mean age for first hospitalization was 23 years, and the average stay was 11 months. The most frequent diagnosis was schizophrenia (39%), followed by affective disorder (20%).

A 1991 study (Unger et al.) compared demographic and clinical data of supported education students ($N = 52$) with other large groups of individuals diagnosed with mental illness ($N = 1,328$). The large groups were composed of individuals who were enrolled in community support or psychosocial programs. The supported education students were younger, more likely to have had some college education, less likely to have been married, and more likely to have worked in the past 5 years. The students on average were more likely to have been hospitalized. Their hospitalizations tended to be for longer periods of time than those of the people in the community support programs but were for shorter periods than those of the psychosocial program participants. They also were less likely to have a diagnosis of schizophrenia.

Mental health clients who return to college often have a history of mental illness that traces back 12–15 years. These individuals often experience a developmental lag in social and vocational skills and may lack experience in daily living that most young adults possess. Research has shown, however, that a psychiatric illness does not necessarily interfere with learning if the symptoms are managed by medication and a supportive lifestyle (Wilson, 1996). By law, every individual has the right to attend a postsecondary institution if he or she meets the institution's admission standards. Therefore, whoever wishes to return to school should have the opportunity to pursue his or her education goals.

SUPPORTED EDUCATION SERVICES

Supported education is a relatively new service option, and many mental health providers are uncertain as to the skills they need to provide this option effectively. The core of supported education services is case management skills. Practitioners need to know how to help consumers develop an education goal, conduct an assessment of service needs, develop an education/service plan, teach skills, link people with services, monitor the student's use of the skills and services, provide support, and evaluate the student's progress. However, these are traditional skills that are now simply being applied in a new environment—postsecondary education. Most practitioners have had experience working in the college environment because they have spent at least 4 years earning their own degrees. Although it does take time to learn the idiosyncrasies of different colleges or training programs in different geographic areas, there is a familiar territory.

Although case management skills are essential to a successful supported education program, the attitudes of the staff, the culture of the organization or agency, and an informal support network made up of peers and family are equally important. The attitudes of the staff can convey hope, despair, encouragement, or apathy. People who have experienced a mental illness often need to be encouraged to shrug off the common stereotypical role of "mental health consumer." They often have been told that their futures will be very limited. They may need help to see themselves in a new more productive role. Mental health staff can be instrumental in helping these individuals develop a new image of themselves. Many individuals have attributed the start of their recovery to a professional who believed in them and encouraged them to trust their own judgment and follow their own dreams. Staff attitudes and beliefs regarding their clients can have a very significant effect on how their clients progress.

The culture of an agency or organization also can have a significant effect on progress. If the culture supports a "we" versus "them" attitude, distance is created and maintained between the staff and the clients. Differences are exaggerated and emphasized. If the culture supports an attitude that everyone is important and special and that staff and clients have more similarities than differences, the supportive relationships that are vital to recovery can be developed and nurtured.

Part of the day-to-day operations of an agency should include opportunities for individuals to explore their options and capabilities as well as celebrate their progress and milestones. Although these individuals benefit immensely from learning new skills and gaining new knowledge, they also learn contextually. The director of a hospital program was astonished when individuals in a locked ward behaved like "normal" students when they were provided with a classroom and a teacher and were expected to learn. The students modified their behavior to match the context of the situation. This is the kind of opportunity that should be available every day. Clients also learn about returning to school from their interaction with clients who are already enrolled. Similarly, they learn about work from consumers who are employed.

Activities to intermingle with people in the community should be commonplace. Having a celebration in a local church with church members gives individuals a renewed sense of themselves. It says not only that they have accomplished something but also that their progress makes a difference to others.

Professional support and intervention are a vital part of the services that make up an environment to enhance rehabilitation and recovery. Equally important is the relationship clients have with their peers. Emotional support from friends, encouragement, and problem solving—all part of human relationships—should be encouraged. In most instances, when given the opportunity, many clients say they prefer to go to their friends for help rather than consult professionals.

Staff attitudes, a recognition of the importance of contextual learning, and an understanding of the value of friendships help an agency build a culture that promotes learning, self-confidence, and recovery. The following are steps that will specifically develop an environment in which consumers see themselves as potential students and workers.

Changing Expectations

Many mental health providers see their role in terms of simply providing clinical services, including medication management, day treatment or rehabilitative services, and case management to keep people safe and healthy. They may not assist their consumers in developing career goals or getting training and education to better their potential for achieving their goals. Work opportunities that many agencies make available are often entry-level or service jobs. Although this work may be appropriate for some individuals, others aspire to careers that more fully utilize their aptitudes and talents. Having career aspirations after a major mental illness is a radical idea in some environments for both practitioners and clients. It requires a major shift in how clients are viewed, by both their providers and themselves. Changing expectations becomes the first step in providing supported education services.

Changing one's expectations does not require a new program or additional funding. It can begin with questions and conversations. Such questions should be related to the individual's hopes for building a more fulfilling and more productive life. Several questions might include the following:

- Do you have dreams for how you want your life to be?
- Do you want to go to work?
- Where do you want to live?
- Who do you want as your friends?
- What are your thoughts about going to work or continuing your education?

Through dialogue, people can arrive at conclusions about themselves. The conversations are sharing experiences that relate to the individual's frame of reference and aspirations. The purpose of the conversations is to expand the consumer's horizons. Many people with a mental illness have been told that their lives are over—that they might as well forget about their dreams. One of the roles of today's providers is to talk about possibilities. Although the client's aspirations may have changed because of his or her illness, he or she still needs to plan his or her life to be as fulfilling and productive as possible. Returning to school is often a first step. If the agency cannot provide complete supported education services for their clients, then they can encourage them to have education as a goal. The agency can incorporate some of the services needed by rethinking case management services or changing the content of day treatment programs.

Developing a Goal   An important step in planning a more meaningful life is for the client to develop goals. This process can be accomplished in a group setting with individual follow-up, or it can be conducted one-to-one. Goals stem from a person's desire for something and should be based on values and needs. Examples of education goals might include the following:

- To complete an Associate in Arts degree in 4 years
- To upgrade math and language skills to a twelfth-grade level
- To complete a training certificate in drug and alcohol counseling
- To complete a 4-year degree at a university with a major in psychology

There are many formal and informal surveys or assessments for helping consumers to explore their values. Because many people lose a sense of self-identity when they develop a mental illness, developing goals is a helpful way for them to learn more about who they are now.

Another way to gather information is to discuss the person's previous experiences in school. What worked well? What presented difficulties? What did the person enjoy doing? Does the person like to be with people? Does the person prefer working with ideas or things? What are the person's abilities? People learn from being with others. If consumers in the agency are working or going to school, other consumers can learn from them when they hear them talk about their experiences and see them going off to their jobs or classes.

Although many schools provide testing so that students can be placed in appropriate classes, it is often helpful to assess their basic academic skills before they go to school. The Wide-Range Achievement Test–Revised (Wilkinson, 1993) or similar tests can determine areas that need remediation. A student's level of achievement or academic skills will help determine the most recommended path toward his or her goals.

Another important factor in establishing a meaningful goal is exploring the requirements of the career in which the person has expressed interest. Consumers can do research at their local libraries, conduct informational interviews with people who work in the field, or examine the *Dictionary of Occupational Titles* (U.S. Department of Labor, 1994) to learn more about career opportunities in the area they have chosen. For example, one student wanted to be an attorney. When he researched all of the requirements, including 3 years in law school, he still decided on a career in the field of law but chose to work as a legal advocate rather than as a lawyer.

Not all students scale down their goals. An informal survey (Unger, 1997) indicated that about 6% of students in supported education programs transfer from community colleges to 4-year colleges and universities. A number of people have begun or have completed graduate school. Each student, however, must set goals according to his or her own set of requirements, abilities, and attributes.

Assessing the Needs After a person's goals have been developed and stated, the practitioner works with him or her to assess the skills and resources that are necessary in achieving these goals. Are remedial skills such as reading and arithmetic needed? Does the student need to improve his or her social skills? Does he or she need to learn time management and/or study skills? Has he or she learned how to manage his or her symptoms?

Resources or support service needs also must be assessed. Does the student need financial aid? Help with documenting his or her dis-

ability? Help with registration? Help with getting vocational rehabilitation services? A new therapist or new medication? Personal support?
Crisis intervention?

Developing the Education/Service Plan   The educa-
tion/service plan includes documentation in terms of who is responsible for providing services and where, when, and how these services
will be provided. The plan guides both the practitioner and the consumer when deciding what needs to be accomplished for the student
to be successful. Developing the service plan requires that the practitioner and the student determine which resources are available in the
agency and the community (including the student's school) and how
each will be used (see Table 7.1).

Teaching Skills   Many mental health agencies develop pro-
grams that help people return to college. The classes available within
such programs include remedial math and English, computer skills,
career exploration, time management, symptom management, stress
reduction, nutrition and exercise, peer support, and using community
resources. The classes can be taken on a rotating or ongoing basis or
during the summer. Many of the classes, particularly symptom management, are helpful to all mental health consumers. In addition, once
clients enroll in school, they may need tutors to help them with their
classwork. Some mental health agencies arrange for staff or other
clients to assist these individuals.

Students need a variety of skills to adjust to the school environment. Some of the needed skills, such as commuting and parking,
are very practical and concrete. Other skills are more interpersonal
(e.g., getting along with others) and intrapersonal (e.g., managing
your own behavior). Many of these skills can be taught in a mental
health setting, and staff can coach their clients through the process of

Table 7.1.   An education/service plan

Priority	Needed	Who	When	Where
1	Developing an educational goal	Counselor/ student	8/1	MH Agency
2	Financial aid	DS office/FAO	9/10	College
3	Selecting classes	DS office/student	9/15	College
4	Study skills	Peer tutor	9/21	MH Agency
5	Accommodation for testing	DS/instructor	9/29	Classroom
6	Tutoring for math	Tutor	9/29	MH Agency
7	Making friends	Instructor/peers	9/21	MH Agency

Note: MH, mental health; DS, Disability Service; FAO, Financial Aid Office.

using them on campus. Some of the skills students need include the following:

- Commuting to campus
- Maneuvering around campus
- Using administrative services (e.g., getting a transcript)
- Applying for financial aid
- Selecting and registering for classes
- Using the college resources (e.g., library, learning center)
- Clarifying assignments
- Managing time
- Taking notes
- Completing assignments
- Preparing for and taking tests
- In-class participation
- Asking and answering questions
- Managing internal distractions (e.g., voices, negative thoughts)
- Meeting with college staff (e.g., professors, advisors)
- Managing emotions
- Coping strategies for feelings and symptoms associated with the illness
- Responding to feedback
- Meeting people (i.e., making friends)
- Listening
- Managing free time on campus (Walsh, Sharac, & Sullivan, 1990, p. 48)

Linking to Resources Linking to resources is not simply making a telephone call. It includes determining the student's specific values and preferences in relation to using a resource. For example, if a student needs a new therapist, what are the most important qualities for the therapist to possess? If a student is looking for a stress reduction class in the community, what are the most important characteristics (e.g., the time the program meets, the duration of the program, the program's content) for which to look?

Identifying community resources requires some knowledge of the community. Much of this information can be found in the yellow pages, newspapers, directories, and the local library. Part of linking to resources is determining who makes up the client's natural support system. It also is important to determine what resources will be available to students with mental illness on the college campus and what support services the mental health agency will provide.

Monitoring Provision of Services One of the characteristics of students with a mental illness who return to school is that they often require more support initially than other students. Because they often lack self-esteem and self-confidence and are fearful of new experiences, they may need help in feeling more comfortable and confident. They may not have mastered some social and interpersonal skills. (Their prevocational and basic work skills may not be as developed as other students' skills.) They often are more similar to other returning adult students than are young adults just out of high school.

One way to help individuals through the initial adjustment of returning to school is to provide personal support. This can be accomplished simply by being there when a person wants to talk about his or her experiences. It also is helpful if students know that when they are on campus they can call the mental health agency and talk to someone who is concerned and interested in their progress.

Some mental health staff will accompany students to campus or to class until they know their way around and feel more comfortable. If an agency has a supported education program, on-campus support may be available during certain hours of the day. If an agency has clients in several schools, staff members may travel from campus to campus and provide support where they are needed. (See Chapter 1 for a discussion of models of supported education.)

Evaluating Services Practitioners should evaluate each student's education/service plan to determine whether the plan is being followed or whether it needs to be revised. The effectiveness of the various interventions should be assessed to see if the client's needs are being met. Evaluation can be an informal process accomplished through conversations with the client, but it should be ongoing nonetheless. Changes need to be made if expectations are not being met. Because of the vulnerability of many individuals, particularly as they initially return to campus, they can be derailed by many experiences, demands, or circumstances.

GUIDELINES FOR REFERRING CONSUMERS TO COLLEGE DISABILITY SERVICES OFFICES

During the development of the service plan, it is helpful for the student to introduce themselves to the disability services (DS) counselor and gather information on what is needed to qualify for services and learn about the services that are offered. The following are guidelines for mental health staff when referring a student to a DS office:

- Call the DS office for the name of the person to see. Advise them that a referral has been made.
- Offer to attend the initial meeting with the consumer.
- Prepare the consumer to share his or her education goals with the DS counselor.

- Prepare the consumer to talk with the DS counselor about any needs for support or accommodations he or she may have because of his or her disability.
- Clarify the role of a mental health service provider, and determine who will do what to support the student (Project GEO, 1997).

GUIDELINES FOR ASSISTING STUDENTS WHO ATTEND COLLEGE

Some mental health agencies have begun training programs to help mental health consumers return to school. These programs aim to increase the opportunity for employment, and education is a step in working toward that goal. The training in these programs emphasizes building connections with many segments of the community so that the widest possible range of opportunities are available to individuals with psychiatric disabilities. Mental health staff are encouraged to work closely with college personnel. The following guidelines are for mental health providers who would like to assist their clients in returning to school:

- Take an interest in your clients' education.
- Assist your clients in coordinating their education plans with their service plans and goals.
- Establish and maintain a liaison with the college DS counselors.
- Determine with your clients and the DS counselors what skills and supports your clients will need and who will provide them.
- Develop a service delivery plan with your clients and DS counselors.
- Assist your clients in modifying their home environments to help themselves study.
- Monitor your clients' progress regularly and facilitate their modifications of supports when indicated.
- Hold team meetings with your clients and their providers to assess progress or to intervene if necessary.
- Encourage your clients to call their DS counselors immediately if they must miss school as a result of illness or hospitalization.
- Assist your clients in obtaining school work or assignments if they miss school as a result of illness.
- Assist your clients to call their DS counselors immediately if they decide to drop any or all classes. Encourage your clients to include the mental health providers and the DS counselors in their decisions related to their education plan (Project GEO, 1997).

It is important to know that a student must qualify as an individual with a disability in order to receive services from the DS office. This means that he or she must document his or her disability and the resulting impairments to qualify for services. Some students choose not to disclose their disabilities because they fear reprisals or unequal treatment. They also may not want to identify themselves as having disabilities. Some students have had difficult experiences when their professors or other students found out that they had a psychiatric disability. Others have felt that they were very well received and were relieved to act and behave as they naturally would (Dougherty et al., 1996). The decision to disclose should be made prior to enrollment. (See Chapter 8 for a discussion on disclosure.)

SUPPORTED EDUCATION AND SUPPORTED EMPLOYMENT

Most mental health agencies recognize the importance of employment programs (of which supported employment may be one option) as part of the range of services that they provide. Some agencies have linked these services together so that they have a dual track—employment and education—available when clients enter the agency or when they are ready. The services are not mutually exclusive, and clients can move between them or do both at the same time (Egnew, 1993, 1997).

Employment programs and education programs share common principles. Although the services provided are not identical, they are very similar, and the same staff could serve in both functions. The 1992 Consensus Statement by the National Institute on Disability and Rehabilitation Research (NIDRR) listed a common set of values that made employment programs successful, which were very similar to the values that also made supported education successful. (See Chapter 1 for a detailed description of the values of supported education.)

> **Consumer choice** Successful programs both value and act on consumer empowerment perspectives, providing consumers . . . as wide a range of choices as possible.
> **Integrated settings** Real work opportunities should be in integrated an environment as possible, in which consumers . . . have maximal opportunities to interact with nondisabled co-workers, supervisors, and the general public.
> **Psychosocial service linkages** Psychosocial rehabilitation agencies promote employment outcomes by providing both work-oriented programs and a range of non-vocational supportive services—housing, financial management, social, etc.—that the consumer may need in order to function effectively on the job.

Natural supports   Many programs have sought to draw upon "natural supports" in the consumer's life—family members, co-workers, mentors, company employee Assistance Programs, etc.—to provide working consumers with the support they need to remain employed.

Rapid placement   Effective programs move consumers on to real jobs in the community quickly, minimizing preplacement preparation. . . .

Job accommodation   Effective support stresses the need for job accommodations, which may be provided either by the employer or by the rehabilitation program.

Continuity of services   "Seamless" services—ongoing programs that do not force shifts of counselors, agency affiliations, or relationships as the consumer moves within the process—are best for consumers.

Pro-active services   Effective programs work pro-actively, encouraging clients early and continuously with regard to their employment prospects. (1992, pp. 16–17)

Choice, integrated settings, linkages, natural supports, rapid placement, accommodations, continuity of services, and proactive services are all elements of a supported education program. Both employment and education programs provide consumers with opportunities to return to their communities and to participate in environments with other workers and students; both acknowledge the importance of services and support to successfully sustain the consumer's activities.

DEVELOPING COMMUNITY COALITIONS

Some of the most successful supported education programs have been developed through the work of community coalitions. By pooling the talents and resources of many staff and agencies, existing resources can be used to develop and implement supported education programs. No new resources are necessarily needed because each agency has its own designated or mandated role and included in that role is working with people with mental illnesses. Supported education coalitions have brought many providers to the table who have never spoken or worked together. Not only are the clients better served but also, through cooperation and sharing, agency staff feel more connected and productive—and resources can be used more effectively.

The most visible partner in supported education programs for mental health agencies is the community college or trade school. Community colleges have been experiencing a large influx of students with a history of mental illness, and staff often feel overwhelmed or ill prepared to work with this new group of students with disabilities. They often welcome a seat at the coalition meetings because collaboration expands their knowledge and resources. In turn, they can provide information about college admission, registration, financial aid, accommodations, and college services. Figure 7.1 shows how agencies can work together to share resources and provide supported education services to the clients in their area.

Each community has its own constellation of agencies and resources. Any person or agency could take the lead in forming a coalition. An individual or an agency needs to keep people on track and working; thus, a leader is important. Initiating a relationship with a

Agency services	College	Mental health agency	Vocational rehabilitation	Housing	Consumer group	National Alliance for the Mentally Ill (NAMI)	Psychiatric hospital
Assessment	✔	✔	✔				✔
Case management		✔		✔			
Counseling	✔	✔	✔				✔
Classes	✔	✔			✔		✔
Crisis intervention		✔					✔
Financial	✔		✔			✔	
Medication		✔					✔
Rehabilitation		✔	✔				
Peer support	✔	✔		✔	✔		
Referral	✔	✔	✔	✔	✔	✔	✔
Instruction	✔	✔		✔	✔		✔
Support	✔	✔	✔	✔			
Tutoring	✔	✔		✔	✔		
Consulting		✔		✔	✔	✔	

Figure 7.1.   Services provided by a coalition of teams.

postsecondary educational institution or any other agency may be a new experience for mental health providers. To enhance the chances of a successful outcome, the following guidelines are suggested:

- Begin at a parallel organizational level.
- Bring another staff member from the agency with you to the meeting.
- Frame your request as part of a larger community/social issue (i.e., the reintegration of people with psychiatric disabilities into the community).
- Do not speak initially of legal responsibilities.
- Come with an open mind (i.e., do not arrive with a solution).
- Listen to and validate the concerns expressed by the college.
- Be prepared to redirect some resources (e.g., staff time) to supported education programs.
- Think about the future. This is the beginning of a long-term relationship (Stringari, 1994).

MODEL PROGRAMS

Many mental health agencies throughout the United States have supported education programs. They exist in a variety of settings. Some are part of community coalitions; others exist independently. The following examples have been chosen to demonstrate the variety of programs and settings that are possible.

A Community Supported Education Program Located at a College

Although the College of San Mateo in San Mateo, California, is not a mental health provider, it has become an integral part of the rehabilitation services available in its community. The Transition to College Program was initiated by the mental health community in response to the lack of services at the college level for its population. However, the program is college based, and all services are provided on campus. The program's mission is to assist individuals whose lives have been interrupted by severe mental illness to attend college, manage their disability, and successfully make the transition from the role of a mental health client to that of a student and/or employee.

Prior to the initiation of the Transition to College Program, few if any special services or accommodations were being offered in community colleges to individuals with psychiatric disabilities. In 1990, a growing mental health consumer movement in San Mateo County,

California, led by the Peninsula Network of Mental Health Clients, the National Alliance for the Mentally Ill (NAMI), the Mental Health Association of San Mateo County, and Caminar (a housing provider), began to focus on the lack of supportive services for people with mental illness to return to college. A coalition was formed and supported by the San Mateo County Mental Health Services; the coalition approached the College of San Mateo to request the development of services and programs.

Faced with budget reductions, the college could not immediately fund new programs but offered to meet with the coalition on an ongoing basis to pool resources and seek outside funding to expand services and develop programs. Soon afterward, the college, assisted by and in cooperation with this coalition, applied for and received funding and technical assistance to develop a model service site.

As of 1998, the program is funded in diverse ways. The college receives reimbursement from the state for providing education and disability-related services. Specialized classes are taught by instructors from Caminar; the County Mental Health Division; and the college. The County Mental Health Division pays the salary of the supported education program counselor, and the County Mental Health Division staff have developed curriculum on peer counseling and symptom management. The California State Department of Rehabilitation provides job counseling on campus and an instructor for a skill development course. The NAMI provides a book scholarship program, and the Mental Health Association has written and administered grants.

Service contributions are made by the Peninsula Network of Mental Health Patients and the National Outreach for Mental Health, a "Stomp Out Stigma" client group that provides speakers for presentations and advises the coalition on consumers' rights. The psychiatric hospital provides crisis intervention services and mobile crisis support. Each member of the Coalition provides or contributes to the program in some way.

Since its inception, the Coalition has grown and changed. It is now called the Association of Mental Health Providers, Consumers, Families, Educators, and Employers for San Mateo County. Its mission is to maintain a formal ongoing relationship to facilitate communication, plan collectively, share resources, develop joint programs and services, collaborate in acquisition of external funds, promote county-wide understanding, and support and empower individuals with psychiatric disabilities to develop and attain personal and economic goals.

The Transition to College Program is staffed by seven part-time staff members who are funded by college funds, Carl D. Perkins Vocational and Applied Technology Education Act of 1990 (PL 101-392)

Funds, local foundation grants, and San Mateo County Mental Health Services. Three to five peer counselors and peer assistants work with staff members in instruction, orientation, registration, and monitoring student progress. Many graduate counseling students have used the Transition to College Program as an internship and have provided valued counseling and mentoring.

In the spring of 1996, the Transition to College Program had 103 participants: 63 continuing students, 10 returning students, and 30 new students. The students' primary diagnoses included schizophrenia/ schizo-affective disorder, depression, and bipolar disorder. The attrition rate was 17%, giving the students in the program a higher rate of retention than the other students at the college. GPAs were usually in the 3.0 or higher range (on a 4-point grade scale). Approximately 6% of the students transferred to 4-year programs, and several went on to graduate school (Howard & Shuman, 1996).

Students are systematically asked to evaluate the program and discuss their feelings about returning to college. Their main concerns when entering the program are centered around prejudice, rejection and ridicule, social interactions with peers and instructors, the cost of books and materials, stress overload, inability to concentrate, fear of failure, and lack of self-confidence.

The students report that sensitivity to these concerns and encouragement provided by staff and peers are the most helpful aspects of the program. Support groups that were led by peers and had disability-related counseling, prescriptive academic programming, courses with special emphases, assistance with financial aid applications, assistance with registration, and special college orientations were ranked as the most helpful accommodations.

Consumers and Alliances United for Supported Education

In the fall of 1991, an individual at a state hospital in Massachusetts requested permission to register for graduate study at a local university. His request was denied, so he contacted the Quincy Human Rights Committee, which was staffed by NAMI members. In investigating whether the hospital had violated the patients' rights, NAMI found that there was interest among other individuals with mental illnesses to return to school. They called a meeting at the mental health center and invited all of the individuals who were interested in returning to school. Over 125 people came to the meeting. To meet this identified need, a group from the local NAMI chapter and consumers, in cooperation with the Department of Mental Health (DMH) of Massachusetts, established the Consumers and Alliance United for Supported Education (CAUSE) program. This program is now located in Quincy, Massachusetts, at the Quincy Mental Health Center.

CAUSE is designed to encourage individuals with psychiatric disabilities to enter or reenter college or technical school programs. Students attend the colleges of their choice either to improve their employment potential or for personal enrichment. Students enroll at 20 various colleges in the greater Boston area. Students range in age from 18 to 60 years and have a primary diagnosis of schizophrenia, depression, or bipolar disorder.

The DMH funds the program, which includes a director who also manages consumer affairs for the DMH, $1^1/_2$ FTE peer counselors, $1^1/_2$ supported education specialists, and a half-time administrative assistant. The program is also staffed by six administrative assistants who are office apprentices, as well as numerous consumer volunteers. The paid staff includes three mental health consumers, a family member, and a nonconsumer provider. Some staff are located on-site at the DMH Office, but supported education specialists also provide mobile support and go where the students need them. Four peer support groups are coordinated by staff on different campuses. CAUSE is overseen by an advisory board composed of NAMI members, community representatives from vocational rehabilitation and mental health agencies, consumers, and staff. All decisions are made on a consensus basis and in accordance with their program mission.

In the spring of 1997, CAUSE supported 107 students who were enrolled in college. It is preparing another 110 students to return to school by helping them with such tasks as choosing a college, finding financial aid, and arranging transportation to and from school. Students who have or are participating in CAUSE have a higher retention rate than the other students and maintain higher-than-average grades. Of the 107 students attending college, 42 are enrolled in degree-granting programs.

CAUSE provides academic and career counseling, assistance with registration and financial aid, advocacy, and information and referral. Students also can receive help with notetaking, study skills, and completing assignments; staff will tutor and coach students and proctor exams. CAUSE will also help the student determine the accommodations he or she may need and advocate for the students with the college.

Other notable activities supported by CAUSE include the Consumer University (Consumer U), which is a program developed for and by consumers to develop readiness and teach self-management courses. The courses include co-counseling, advocacy, benefit specialists, crisis counseling, and others. Many of the classes are taught by the consumers themselves. There is also an outreach program to encourage local church congregations to join in welcoming and encouraging the participation of people with a history of mental illness to become part of their congregations.

A Supported Education Program in a Clubhouse

Laurel House in Stamford, Connecticut, a clubhouse modeled after Fountain House in New York, began a supported education program in the early 1980s using the philosophy of supported employment. Where Laurel House had previously helped people through the employment office to find employment, they now developed a program to assist students with admissions, financial aid, and enrollment (Dougherty, 1997).

Laurel House also provides ongoing support to its members while they are in school. Staff found that the support role for education was essentially the same as the support role for employment, although they needed to learn the admissions and registration processes and establish relationships with school personnel.

After students are enrolled, Laurel House students usually receive academic support from the colleges they attend through the DS office. They are also eligible to receive many other social and academic services, including educational and vocational interests and needs assessments.

Laurel House has one full-time staff person who provides educational support services. This person discusses with members the benefits of returning to school, helps students with registration and financial aid, provides or arranges for tutoring, gives individual help with assignments, and oversees an education support group. In addition, this person travels to the campus if a student needs on-site assistance. Other clubhouse staff provide informal support. Fellow students and other clubhouse members support the educational goals of fellow members, and a culture has developed in which education is as important an option for gaining independence as employment.

As of 1998, 70 members of Laurel House have returned to school, taking more than 300 courses collectively. They have consistently maintained a B+ average. Several members have graduated. A student comment best typifies what it means for a clubhouse member to return to school: "I was walking down the street and met some friends I hadn't seen for awhile. We said 'Hi,' they asked what's new, and I told them I had gone back to college. They were so excited for me. They put their arms around me and hugged me. I was thrilled and very proud" (Clubhouse member, personal communication, 1990).

A Supported Education
Program in a Community Services Agency

The Kennedy Service Center, located in Trumbull, Connecticut, developed a supported employment program in 1989 in collaboration with the state of Connecticut DMH. The program's goal is to offer a pathway for people with psychiatric disabilities to develop their vocational aspirations by exploring, gaining access to, and completing postsecondary educational opportunities (Pettella, Tarnoczy, & Geller, 1996).

The supported education program has three components: preadmission services, support group and summer workshop series, and individualized tutoring and support skills. In order to receive supported education services, the potential candidate is assessed to determine his or her level of motivation and commitment to an education goal. The student's entrance into the program must be approved by the DMH.

In the preadmission process, students are tested for career interests, skills, and abilities. They must articulate a long-term vocational goal and relate this goal to their education plan. This exploration process is facilitated by program staff. Staff also assist the potential student to match his or her career goal and personal interests to a college or training program and with financial aid planning.

Another service the program offers is a support group that meets monthly at one of the colleges. It is an informal discussion group co-facilitated by the Kennedy Center staff. A series of workshops are offered in the summer, which are geared toward preparing students for the upcoming school year. Workshops offer a video presentation, and guest speakers include graduates of the supported education program.

The third component of the supported education program is individualized tutoring and support skills. Students are assisted with time management, organizational skills, study skills, stress management, individual tutoring, group support, referrals to natural support systems, and other ancillary supports to meet their specific needs. An emphasis is placed on learning skills that will help the student become successful. Techniques such as developing calendars for time management, stress logs, social support charts and inventories, and relaxation techniques are used. There also is a strong emphasis on utilizing the natural supports available on the college campus.

A final characteristic of this program is the use of a consulting psychologist to help staff solve problem situations that may arise with the students. Weekly meetings are used to develop strategies that foster the student's success in school and support the staff in its work of helping students meet their education goals.

In addition to direct services, the program places a strong emphasis on cooperation with the service providers in the students' lives. In-service instruction to schools and other agencies increases service providers' knowledge regarding students with psychiatric disabilities and these students' needs. The program also supports collaboration among the postsecondary schools, the state of Connecticut DMH, the State of Connecticut Bureau of Rehabilitation, and social/recreational clubhouses.

A Supported Education Program in a Hospital Setting

The Western State Hospital Patient and Family Education program is a contracted program through Pierce Community College, located in Tacoma, Washington. It has provided education services to individuals in the Western State Hospital since the mid-1970s. When the program first began, it was not widely believed that individuals in the hospital could learn because of their mental illness nor was it believed that they would go back to work once they left the hospital. However, Gilmur, who developed the program, said, "Consumers who were highly symptomatic on the wards, were extremely cogent, focused and student-like in the classroom" (1997, p. 29).

The program serves the gamut of the hospital population—adults with psychiatric disorders, forensic patients, older adults, and those in the residential program (Gilmur, 1997). The program has grown to include several tracks: Adult Basic Education and high school completion/general equivalency diploma; psychoeducational classes, including health and wellness, women's health issues, medication education, human immunodeficiency virus/acquired immunodeficiency syndrome; substance abuse; and empowerment, including symptom management and recovery and family/consumer illness education.

The program is staffed by six state-certified instructors, a director, and an office assistant. Approximately 500 individuals are enrolled in education classes quarterly, which is 62% of the individuals in the hospital. Much of the curriculum has been developed by the staff of the program. The teaching methods employed are similar to those used with students with learning disabilities. They include multimodality teaching, repetition, reducing stimuli, experiential learning, and individualized instruction.

For students who want to continue their college education when they leave the hospital, a support program has been developed at Pierce College and is staffed by a program coordinator and an instructor, both of whom are former mental health clients. A mentor program is also

being developed to match each student with a mentor. The Director of
the supported education program said the following:

> I have learned that consumers can benefit from education and the educa-
> tion process, no matter where they are in the process of recovery. They can
> and do learn and thrive on the hopefulness and promise inherent in edu-
> cation . . . they have the right to the full gamut of educational options and
> possibilities available at any time they express the desire. They do not
> have to reach an arbitrary level of "wellness." In fact, education, whether
> it be hospital or community based seems to be intrinsically tied to the
> recovery process for many consumers. (Gilmur, 1997, p. 30)

SUMMARY

There are many positive outcomes in providing supported education
services to people with psychiatric disabilities. A major outcome is that
mental health consumers become college students. The role of college
student is highly valued in American society. The role of mental health
consumer is very devalued. With this change in role and identity, students begin to realize they are not their illness but functioning, productive members of their communities. Although attending college can
increase stress, the stress can be managed with support and a plan for
managing symptoms. The decision to return to school often comes
from improved health, a weariness of the role of mental health client,
and a desire to overcome the diagnosis. That decision and corresponding goal development gives new energy and hope to people with mental illnesses.

REFERENCES

Anonymous. (1990, October). Mental health community news. *DMH Now*, 1–4.
Carl D. Perkins Vocational and Applied Technology Education Act of 1990,
  PL 101-392, 104 Statutes at Large 753–804, 806–834.
Dougherty, S. (1997). A chance to go to school. *The Journal of the California
  Alliance for the Mentally Ill, 8*(2), 36–38.
Dougherty, S., Kampana, K., Kontos, R., Flores, M., Lockhart, R., & Shaw, D.
  (1996). Supported education: A qualitative study of the student experience.
  Psychiatric Rehabilitation Journal, 19(3), 59–70.
Egnew, R.C. (1993). Supported education and employment: An integrated
  approach. *Psychosocial Rehabilitation Journal, 17*(1), 123–127.
Egnew, R. C. (1997). Integrating supported education and supported employ-
  ment. *The Journal of the California Alliance for the Mentally Ill, 8*(2), 33–35.
Gilmur, D. (1997). A hospital based education program: The sequel to commu-
  nity supported education. *The Journal of the California Alliance for the Mentally
  Ill, 8*(2), 28–30.
Hoffman, F., & Mastrianni, X. (1993). The role of supported education in the inpatient treatment of young adults: A two-site comparison. *Psychosocial Rehabilitation Journal, 17*(1), 109–120.

Howard, D., & Shuman, S. (1996). *Transition to college program: The status of new, returning and continuing students for spring, 1996 semester.* San Mateo, CA: College of San Mateo.

National Institute on Disability and Rehabilitation Research (NIDRR). (1992). *Consensus statement: Strategies to secure and maintain employment for people with long term mental illness, 1*(3), Washington, DC: Author.

Pettella, C., Tarnoczy, D.L., & Geller, D. (1996). Supported education: Functional techniques for success. *Psychiatric Rehabilitation Journal, 20*(1), 36–41.

Project GEO. (1997). *Building employment and community connections: A values-based training curriculum for serving people with psychiatric disabilities.* San Francisco: University of San Francisco, Rehabilitation Administration, McLaren Graduate School of Management.

Risser, P. (1992). An empowering journey. *The Journal of the California Alliance for the Mentally Ill, 3*(2), 38–39.

Rogers, S., Walsh, D., Masotta, L., & Danley, K. (1991). *Massachusetts survey of client preferences for community support services final report to Massachusetts Department of Mental Health.* Boston: Boston University, Center for Psychiatric Disabilities.

Stringari, T. (1994). *Recommendations for initiating relationships with your local community colleges.* San Mateo, CA: College of San Mateo, Transition to College Program for People with Psychiatric Disabilities.

Unger, K. (1993). Creating supported education programs utilizing existing community resources. *Psychosocial Rehabilitation Journal, 17*(1), 11–23.

Unger, K. (1996). *Annual performance report to NIDRR on supported education project.* Tucson: University of Arizona, Community Rehabilitation Division.

Unger, K. (1997). *Annual performance report to NIDRR on supported education project.* Tucson: University of Arizona, Community Rehabilitation Division.

Unger, K., Anthony, W., Sciarappa, K., & Rogers, E.S. (1991). Development and evaluation of a supported education program for young adults with long-term mental illness. *Hospital and Community Psychiatry, 42*(8), 838–842.

U.S. Department of Labor. (1994). *Dictionary of occupational titles.* Washington, DC: Author.

Walsh, D., Sharac, J., & Sullivan, A. (1990). *College survival skills: Students with psychiatric disabilities.* Boston: Boston University, Center for Psychiatric Rehabilitation.

Wilkinson, G.S. (1993). *Wide Range Achievement Test–Revised (WRAT–3).* Wilmington, DE: Jastak Associates.

Wilson, M. (1996). Dual diagnosis of psychological and learning disabilities: The role of psychotropic medication in assessment and treatment of learning disabilities. Need editors? *Issues in Psychological Disabilities* (pp. 8–9). Columbus, OH: Association on Higher Education and Disability.

Funding
Supported Education

Kim is not unlike any other student. . . . She is a thirty year old social work major who is not only attending college, but working part-time. She is also a single parent raising a son, with the attendant worries that are involved. She is on financial aid and has no health insurance. She uses our student health services when we are lucky enough to have a psychiatrist on board for a few hours a week. Our pharmacy provides her lithium at cost and, with careful budgeting, she gets by. (Feinberg, 1997, p. 64)

The closest music therapy program to Santa Barbara was one at California State University, Northridge—an hour and a half to the south. It was decided that I would begin the two year program and commute two to three days a week. It was all totally funded by the Department of Rehabilitation. And the whole venture would have been impossible without the emotional support from my case workers, psychiatrist, psychologist and from a disabled student program counselor at CSUN. (Glater, 1992, p. 22)

Funding for supported education services is available through established funding sources for individuals, educational institutions, and agencies. For students with psychiatric disabilities, the general categories of financial aid include grants, loans, and eligibility programs. For educational institutions, financial aid is usually available through avenues set up to serve students with disabilities. For agencies, sources of financial aid vary depending on the state, the county, or the town/city. Each of these funding levels are discussed in this chapter.

FUNDING FOR STUDENTS

There are a number of ways that students with psychiatric disabilities can obtain funding for college, all of which are available to all students through the financial aid offices of postsecondary institutions. Certain funds, however, are earmarked for students with exceptional need. Financial aid resources are scholarships, federal grants, the federal work study (FWS) program, and federal loans. Additional sources of funding are eligibility programs, which include Social Security and Vocational Rehabilitation (VR).

Financial Aid Resources

Financial aid is available for students who do not have the resources to adequately finance their educational expenses. Aid is based on a partnership among the students; the postsecondary educational institution; the states and federal government; private resources; and, in some instances, the VR agency and Social Security Administration. The need for financial aid is determined by the difference between the cost of a student's education (e.g., tuition, books, living expenses) and the amount of money the student can afford to pay. The larger the difference is between these two variables, the more financial aid that may be available.

To establish the need for aid, colleges use a formula established by the U.S. Congress called the Expected Family Contribution (EFC). EFC is the amount the student and his or her family are expected to contribute based on their income. Because most students who return to school after a mental illness are independent, the parent's contributions are usually not considered. Students should apply for financial support through the financial aid office of the institution they plan to attend.

All students applying for financial assistance are required to complete the Free Application for Federal Student Aid (FAFSA). The form requests information on the student's assets, including income and savings. If the student is under 24 years of age, dependent, and living with his or her parents, then the parents must disclose their assets.

The FAFSA also requests the estimated cost of the education. Each school will have available, usually through the school catalog or financial aid office, the estimated costs of attending that institution. The expenses include tuition and fees, supplies needed for coursework, books, living expenses (primarily for room and board), and a moderate amount of money for personal and miscellaneous expenses.

Students with psychiatric disabilities should include in their anticipated expenses any disability-related costs such as special equipment (e.g., tape recorders), special services (e.g., notetakers), and medical expenses directly related to the disability that are not covered by insurance. The special equipment or services necessary because of the disability may be available through either the college or the state VR agency. However, it is important that the financial aid administrator know about the anticipated expenses. These costs will be considered in the determination of the student's financial need, on which all aid decisions are made.

It also is important to understand that disability-related expenses covered by other assisting agencies cannot also be covered by financial aid from the school. For example, if the student is receiving VR services and the agency is funding the costs of tuition and books, the school will not consider those expenses in determining financial aid.

Documentation must be provided to verify the disability. Depending on the institution, documentation may be a written statement from a qualified professional, such as a psychiatrist or VR counselor (see Chapter 5). To be certain what is required, the student should check with the financial aid office.

The student must reapply for financial aid each year through the Renewal FAFSA. This form includes preprinted information from the initial application, spaces for corrections to the original information, and other specific questions that must be answered each year. There is no cost to the student for applying for aid through the Renewal FAFSA.

The application process should be done as early as possible to ensure proper consideration. Errors may result in costly delays or loss of priority status. Help for this rather complicated process is often available through the Disability Services (DS) office or through a case manager at a mental health agency. Financial aid officers are also very helpful.

After a student completes an undergraduate degree, he or she is no longer eligible for certain sources of federal and state funds. VR is particularly reluctant to provide funds for postgraduate work because there is an expectation of employment after graduation from an undergraduate college. However, students who wish to attend graduate school can use the traditional routes of institutional scholarships in the field of study (e.g., loans, part-time or alternate semester employment, family contributions) as financial support for the graduate degree. The graduate school or academic department can provide information about funding.

Scholarships   Scholarships are part of the financial aid package that may be offered to an undergraduate student through the FAFSA application process. Most postsecondary institutions have their own scholarship programs in addition to those available through state and federal funding. Some states also may grant tuition waivers for students who qualify as low-income students. Additional sources of scholarships can be found through scholarship search services; the Internet; and service clubs such as the Kiwanis Club, the Elks Grand Lodge, Rotary Club, the Lions Club, and the National Association of American Business Clubs. Local libraries often have resource books that provide detailed information about scholarships. Scholarships may vary depending on whether a college is a 2- or 4-year institution, state funded, or private.

Federal Grants   Federal grants are another source of funding available for students with disabilities. They include Pell grants and Federal Supplemental Educational Opportunity grants (FSEOGs).

Pell grants are awarded to undergraduate students who have not earned a bachelor's or a professional degree. Pell grants do not have to be repaid. To qualify, a student must complete a financial aid application and demonstrate that the cost of the education exceeds his or her ability to pay. The amount received in aid will depend on the cost of going to school, the student's resources, whether he or she is a full- or part-time student, and whether he or she attends school for an entire academic year. The maximum award for the 1996–1997 award year was $2,470. A school can apply Pell grant funds to the school costs or pay the student directly (usually by check), or combine these methods. The school must notify the student in writing how and when he or she will be paid.

FSEOGs are another federal gift/aid program for undergraduate students with exceptional financial need. Pell grant recipients with the lowest EFCs will be the first students to get FSEOGs, which also are not repaid. A student may receive from $100 to $4,000 a year, depending on when he or she applies, his or her financial need, and the funding level of the school. Money from a FSEOG is dispersed in the same manner as Pell grants.

The Federal Work Study (FWS) Program   The FWS program provides part-time jobs for undergraduate and graduate students with financial need so they may earn money to help pay educational expenses. The program encourages on-campus or community service work and work related to the student's course of study. FWS students are paid by the hour, and the wages must be equal to at least the current federal minimum wage but may be higher, depending on the type of work done and the skills required.

When assigning work hours, the employer or financial aid administrator will consider the student's total award amount, his or her class schedule, and his or her academic progress. If the student works on campus, he or she usually will work for the school. If he or she works off campus, the employer will usually be a private, nonprofit organization or a public agency. The work performed must be in the public interest.

Federal Loans   Unless a student has been successful in college and maintained both a good grade point average and strong full- or part-time status, it is not recommended that he or she consider loans. It takes some students several semesters to develop the endurance and work habits necessary to complete a degree program. This developmental process should be considered when applying for a financial aid package.

Federal Perkins Loans   Federal Perkins Loans are low-interest loans for both undergraduates and graduate students with exceptional financial need. Federal Perkins Loans are made through a school's financial aid office and must be repaid. A student can borrow up to $3,000 for each year of undergraduate study. The total amount a student can borrow as an undergraduate is $15,000. If a payment is missed or if less than a full payment is made, a late fee and collection cost may be charged. Repayment must begin 9 months after graduation, if the student leaves school, or if he or she drops below half-time status. Students have up to 10 years to repay the loan in full.

Direct and Federal Family Education Loans   Direct and Federal Family Education Loans are the Department of Education's major form of self-help aid. They may be subsidized or unsubsidized. An unsubsidized loan is not awarded on the basis of financial need. Interest is charged from the time the loan is disbursed until it is paid in full. A subsidized loan is awarded on the basis of financial need, and interest will not be charged until repayment is begun or during authorized periods of deferments. These loans provide substantial amounts of money for students who are fully matriculated in a program of study that is at least a full academic year. The financial aid administrator of the educational institution will be able to provide details regarding application, disbursement, and repayment.

Eligibility Programs

Eligibility programs are programs for which a person must qualify based on need. Two eligibility programs that are available to students with psychiatric disabilities are VR and Social Security. To receive services, students must meet eligibility requirements that include verification of disability and need. Each agency has different requirements.

Vocational Rehabilitation Agencies   VR agencies have
undergone a change since 1992 as a result of the Rehabilitation Act
Amendments of 1992 (PL 102-569) and the implementation of new regulations. The results of these changes have helped VR agencies to become more accessible to their clients and more responsive to their
clients' individual needs. One of the major changes among VR agencies
has been the reduction in the time and effort required to determine eligibility. A second change is an attempt to work more in partnership
with the individuals in determining their service needs and methods of
service provision.

To receive services from a VR agency, the following steps are
necessary. First, a VR counselor will determine eligibility. Eligibility is
based on three criteria:

1.   The person requesting services must have a verifiable disability.
2.   The disability must result in an impairment to obtaining and main-
     taining employment.
3.   The person must require VR services to become employed.

The ability to benefit from the services is no longer a criterion for
receiving services as it had been in the past. It is assumed that if the
person is there and is willing to work, then he or she is able to benefit
unless there is convincing evidence to the contrary.

Verification of the disability may be established through existing
records, often eliminating a long period of assessment. If existing medical and employment records are not available or are inadequate, an
assessment process may be necessary; but the average time for the
assessment has decreased substantially. It is possible, with proper documentation, to begin the development of an individualized education
program in the first several visits.

An individualized employment plan provides a blueprint for the
services to be provided. It is developed by the counselor and the consumer and guided by consumer choice. The plan includes the development of an employment goal, the identification of the services and
resources needed to meet the goal, and the identification of the service
providers. An exploration of different job options may be included in
the plan, including a process for job shadowing. Although all decisions
are driven by consumer preferences, they are influenced by the policies
of the VR agency and the jobs and resources available in the community. Because the primary goal of the VR counselor is to assist the consumer to become employed, the language of the plan is very important
and must reflect the goal of going to work. Returning to school is an
interim step toward attaining the employment goal.

If it is determined in the goal-setting process that returning to school is a necessary step to reaching the employment goal, a VR agency may assist the person with his or her education by providing tuition assistance, transportation, books, reader services, or other individually prescribed aids and devices that have been included in the employment plan. Services may differ from state to state, depending on the policies and resources of each state agency.

The development of the individualized employment plan is a collaborative effort between the counselor and the consumer. It is helpful if the consumer approaches the counselor with a clear goal in mind and an attitude of cooperation. Although the counselors are mandated to provide services, an attitude of collaboration and cooperation may produce a plan that is more satisfactory to the consumer.

VR offices and each postsecondary institution's Office of Financial Aid work closely together to determine the aid that will be available to individual students. Because VR agencies, colleges, and universities receive federal money, there can be no overlap of service dollars. Students served by a VR agency who are planning to return to school as full- or part-time students or for more than one or two classes are required to apply for student financial aid. Because the process can be complicated, it is important that it be started as early as possible.

Social Security Social Security is a safety net for those people who are unable to work because of a disability. People are considered to have a disability if they are unable to do any kind of work for which they are suited and if the disability is expected to last for at least 1 year or to result in death. Social Security is available only if all other resources have been expended. Benefits continue as long as the person continues to have the disability.

People who believe they are eligible for Social Security should apply as soon as they can. Most towns or cities have offices, but the application can also be made by mail or by telephone. Social Security benefits will not begin until the sixth month of disability. This "waiting period" begins with the first full month after it was determined that the person was eligible.

The process for receiving benefits may take from 60 to 90 days. Part of the process is determining eligibility. Some of the documents required for eligibility include detailed medical records, medications taken, employment summary for the past 15 years, and W-2 tax forms. Final determination is made by the Disability Determination Services office in each state. If a person is determined to be eligible for Social Security assistance, he or she will receive both cash payments and Medicare, which provides hospital and medical insurance.

Under regular Social Security rules, Social Security benefits are reduced by other income. However, if the person receiving the benefits wishes to return to work but feels he or she needs to return to school before getting a job, the individual can develop a Plan for Achieving Self-Support (PASS).

PASS allows a student who is eligible for Supplemental Security Income (SSI), or in some cases Social Security Disability Insurance, to set aside money to help him- or herself achieve a work goal. If the person wants to return to school, the plan may be used to pay for tuition, fees, books, and supplies that are needed for school or instruction. The money set aside will not reduce the SSI benefit and does not count against that person's $2,000 resource limit. The goal of a PASS program must be a job that will produce sufficient earnings to reduce dependency on SSI payments. PASS is meant to help acquire the items, skills, or services needed to compete in a professional, business, or trade environment.

People who have a PASS must 1) want to go to work, 2) be eligible for or receive SSI, and 3) expect to receive income (other than SSI) and/or resources to set aside toward a work goal. In order to receive a PASS plan, a work goal must be set; the steps, time, and costs to reach the goal must be determined; and the money set aside for the goal must be accounted for. The plan must be in writing and must be approved by the Social Security Administration. The Social Security office needs to be informed before any changes are made in the plan so the student is not held responsible for payback. A plan may be changed with approval.

Students who are interested in developing a PASS may get help in doing so from a vocational counselor, DS staff, mental health staff, Social Security staff, or friends who have gone through the process. (See the Appendix at the end of this book for complete information for contacting Social Security staff.)

Other Sources of Student Aid   Although the federal government is the largest source of student financial aid, other sources are available. The state higher education agency of each state has information about state aid, including the State Student Incentive Grant, which is jointly funded by individual states and the U.S. Department of Education.

The AmeriCorps program provides full-time educational grants in return for work in community service. Students can work before, during, or after they complete their education. The funds can be used to either pay current educational expenses or repay federal student loans. Aid also may be available from organizations within particular fields. Foundations, religious organizations, fraternities or sororities, or community groups such as the Lions Club, Kiwanis, the American Legion, or the Elks may provide financial assistance to students in their local areas. The public library is also a good source of information for all categories of financial aid. (Refer to the Appendix at the end of this book for additional resources.)

FUNDING FOR POSTSECONDARY EDUCATIONAL INSTITUTIONS

Funding for disability services at postsecondary educational institutions is provided primarily through the institution's general fund and state monies. Every college or university is required to have made provisions for the implementation of Section 504 and the Americans with Disabilities Act (ADA) of 1990 (PL 101-336), usually through the DS Office.

Two other sources of funding are available to increase services for students with disabilities: the TRIO Programs, funded through the Higher Education Act (Steadman, 1997), and the Carl D. Perkins Vocational and Applied Technology Act Amendments of 1990 (PL 101-392) Funds. The purpose of the TRIO Programs is to improve access to postsecondary education for low-income students or students with disabilities who have the potential to become first-generation college students. The U.S. Department of Education awards discretionary grants to higher education institutions for the administration of these programs.

The Carl D. Perkins Vocational and Applied Technology Act Funds support vocational education programs for students with disabilities. It includes funds for vocational assessments, vocational planning, and counseling support as students move through a vocational education program. It is also administered through discretionary grants.

FUNDING FOR MENTAL HEALTH AGENCIES

There is no special funding available to mental health providers for supported education services. However, many agencies have provided the services by reordering service priorities, reallocating resources, and reassigning staff time (Unger, 1993). Examples of how this was done include changing priorities or eliminating one program to put resources into the supported education program, or reassigning staff time so that staff positions could be allocated to a supported education program.

One of the most promising models is to incorporate supported education services into supported employment or vocational services

(Egnew, 1993, 1997). Consumers can develop a single vocational plan, which may include either supported education and/or employment services. Vocational staff can provide both services.

Another model to provide services from a mental health agency is a fee-for-service model (Center for Psychiatric Rehabilitation, 1993). In this model, the agency contracts with potential students to provide support services to them throughout a quarter/semester for a designated fee. The services might include values clarification, goal setting, development of educational opportunities, school placement assistance, skill and resource assessment, planning, tutoring, supportive counseling, and other services as needed. The primary function of the service is to help the potential student choose an education goal, enroll in a school program, and maintain him- or herself in the program until the education goal is achieved. Staff are available to meet at the agency site or to travel and supply support as needed, using a mobile support model.

A third model was demonstrated by the Department of Mental Health (DMH) in Massachusetts (Lim, Nicolellis, Fahey, & Jaggi, 1997). The program included five mental health agencies that served 46 towns. The purpose of the program was to pool financial resources to provide a collaborative service program. It was funded primarily by DMH but received funding support from the agencies that participated in the program to fund a full-time supported education specialist. The specialist assisted the agencies to integrate educational supports into their current day programming and represented the agencies to the educational institutions in the area. Using the mobile support model, the specialist also provided some educational support to students from the five agencies. The agencies provided

- A staff person to help the potential student develop an education goal
- Information about schools/educational opportunities in their area
- Access to financial aid assistance
- Assistance with logistics and transportation related to enrollment
- Education to consumers in their program about returning to school

Supported education services can also be part of a case manager's role. Day treatment programs can include preparatory classes as part of the activities. Some providers have used support services monies from Housing and Urban Development grants to help people return to school. Others have obtained dollars from state VR agencies to provide support services to help people return to work via education.

Another source of program funding comes from in-kind (e.g., staff time, photocopy machines) contributions from community coalitions. (See Chapter 7 for further discussion of this process.)

SUMMARY

There are various funding opportunities available for people with psychiatric disabilities who want to return to school and for the institutions and agencies that support them. Grants, such as Pell grants, are the best option for returning students with psychiatric disabilities until they are well established in the student role. VR services also are a good option if the student is eligible for services.

Funding for educational institutions is usually limited to federal and state funds. However, many colleges have designated certain staff to work specifically with students with psychiatric disabilities, recognizing that the students and the college can benefit from services provided by an understanding and informed college staff person.

The mental health community still has a long way to go in providing routine supported education services for its consumers. Although specific funds are not available, with hope the value of education programs will become as well recognized as the value of employment programs. Both programs support the person's need for a meaningful and productive life.

Supported education services will become increasingly important as more and more people experience the positive results of the new medications that continue to come onto the market. The education environment is an excellent place to regain lost skills and self-esteem, which will make it possible for more people with a history of mental illness to enter the work force.

REFERENCES

Americans with Disabilities Act (ADA) of 1990, PL 101-336, 42 U.S.C. §§ 12101 et seq.

Carl D. Perkins Vocational and Applied Technology Education Act Amendments of 1990, PL 101-392, 104 Statutes at Large 753–804, 806–834.

Center for Psychiatric Rehabilitation. (1993). Career support services. Boston: Boston University.

Egnew, R.C. (1993). Supported education and employment: An integrated approach. Psychosocial Rehabilitation Journal, 17(1), 123–127.

Egnew, R.C. (1997). Integrating supported education and supported employment. The Journal of the California Alliance for the Mentally Ill, 8(2), 33–35.

Feinberg, L.J. (1997). Trial and error: Reflections from a college student with a psychological disability. *The Journal of the California Alliance for the Mentally Ill, 8*(2), 63–64.

Glater, S. (1992). The journey home. *The Journal of the California Alliance for the Mentally Ill, 3*(2), 21–22.

Lim, S., Nicolellis, D., Fahey, H., & Jaggi, C. (1997). *Massachusetts mobile support programs*. Manuscript submitted for publication.

Rehabilitation Act Amendments of 1992, PL 102-569, 29 U.S.C. §§ 101 *et seq.*

Steadman, J.B. (1997, March). CRS report for Congress: Federal TRIO Programs and the National Early Intervention Scholarship and Partnership Program. In *CRS Report for Congress*. Washington, DC: Library of Congress, Congressional Research Service.

Unger, K. (1990, Summer). Supported post secondary education for people with mental illness. *American Rehabilitation*, 10–14.

Unger, K. (1993). Creating supported education programs utilizing existing community resources. *Psychosocial Rehabilitation Journal, 17*(1), 11–23.

Succeeding as a Postsecondary Student

I know that going to school will not give me all the guarantees in the world but it gives me a glimmer of hope, and before, I had no hope whatsoever, and my vision of the future was all black. And just a little hope sometimes is all you need to get by. (Anonymous student, cited in Unger, 1997)

So now I take my medicine. Now I have a job. I'm going to school. I don't want to be sick anymore. I want to be on the other end of the stick where I'm helping others instead of others always helping me. I want to be responsible. (Anonymous student, cited in Unger 1997)

My kids tell me how different I am. I mean they have been trying to get me to go to school forever, and now they call me up and we talk about homework, and you know, its like they're really proud of me that I'm doing this and getting on with my life. (Anonymous student, cited in Unger, 1997)

Returning to school can be both an exciting and an intimidating experience for people who have a history of mental illness: exciting because it marks another beginning, a venture back into the world of learning and new opportunities, and intimidating because of the risks and demands required in a return to an environment that raises questions about ability and acceptance.

Loss of self-esteem and self-confidence are inherent in a diagnosis of mental illness. People with mental illness have often internalized the stigma that surrounds the diagnosis and may not expect to do well in what they perceive as very demanding environments, such as post-secondary schools. They may be overwhelmed by the enormity of the tasks necessary to just enroll, let alone by finding a parking place, the right building, the right office or classroom, and so on. Overcoming fear and self-doubt is difficult and takes enormous strength and energy.

Many people who have been in the mental health system see returning to college as a major turning point in their lives and an opportunity to "get on" with their lives. The opportunity may be prompted by a decrease in symptoms, new medications, better physical health, a change in living situation, or just a time of readiness to try new things. However, it is an anxiety-provoking experience that raises serious questions for many prospective students. Some of the most common questions students raise are

- What should I study?
- Will I be accepted?
- Shall I disclose my disability?
- How will I pay for school?
- What can I do to improve my chances for success?
- Can I manage the stress?
- Will I make friends?
- What if I fail?

In addition to providing some answers to these questions, this chapter offers strategies and resources for promoting student success on campus. However, each student knows him- or herself best and should apply the information that is helpful in a way that works best for him- or herself. These are not simple solutions to complex problems, but the material in this chapter has been helpful to many students.

CHOOSING A FIELD OF STUDY

The decision to return to school should begin with an exploration of the student's values. Questions for the student to answer include the following:

- What do I enjoy doing?
- When am I the happiest?
- What is important to me?
- Do I want to work with people, things, or ideas?

A second set of questions refers to the student's life goals: What do I want my life to look like 1 year from now? Five years from now? Ten years from now?

A second step in determining a field of study is to examine where past success and failure lie. Some questions that the student can ask him- or herself are

- Do I have good people skills?
- Am I good with my hands?
- Am I good with math, and/or do I have technical interests?
- Do I like English and reading, and do I have good verbal skills?
- In which areas have I not been successful?
- What kinds of things do I dislike doing?

Some people have begun college or had a career before the onset of a mental illness. Such experiences will be very helpful in assessing the student's current interests and abilities and determining how to best move forward.

A third step in preparing to go back to school is to examine the time and resources needed to fulfill the student's goal. Questions for the student to ask him- or herself include

- How many years do I want to go to school, and how will I finance my education?
- Do I want to upgrade my current skills?
- Do I want to learn a new trade or a new technical skill?
- Can I meet my goal by attending a community college, a university, or a trade or technical school?
- Do I want a 2-year, a 4-year, or an advanced degree?

All of these questions should be answered when students with psychiatric disabilities are planning to return to school. Vocational Rehabilitation (VR) offices, some mental health services, a peer support group, or the Disability Services (DS) Office may be able to help answer these questions through discussion and various assessment tools. Taking skills assessments prior to enrolling can also help determine classes that are appropriate.

Finding a career exploration class, an orientation to college class, a reentry class, or some class designed to help returning students make the adjustment back into the routine of the learning environment is a good first step for students with psychiatric disabilities to take when beginning the process of returning to school. A few schools, most of which are probably community colleges, may have a special reentry class for people with psychiatric disabilities. Another good way to ease the transition is to take a class such as golf, computer skills, or drawing. Some schools offer classes to upgrade student skills in reading, writing, math, or study skills. There are many ways to attend school without an initial full commitment to a course of study. Although there may be a limited number of classes that can be taken without declaring a major, it is a way to start.

GAINING ACCEPTANCE INTO COLLEGE PROGRAMS AND SERVICES

The Americans with Disabilities Act (ADA) of 1990 (PL 101-336) and Section 504 of the Rehabilitation Act of 1973 (PL 93-112) have made it illegal to deny admission to college programs and services to students with disabilities if they are otherwise qualified. Students with disabilities who apply to an education program cannot be asked to disclose their disability as part of the admission process. The purpose of these laws is to prohibit discrimination. If the student feels he or she has been discriminated against, he or she should contact the compliance office or the ADA coordinator at the college. If the student is unable to locate that office, he or she can contact the Office of Civil Rights (OCR) of the U.S. Department of Education.

Once students are accepted to an institution, they can receive special services and accommodations through DS only if they disclose and document their disability. The documentation must meet certain criteria in order to ensure accommodations (see Chapter 5). This disability-related information must be kept confidential by law and may not be disclosed to instructors or other college personnel, except under special circumstances.

All programs and services are available to all students. If it becomes known that a student has a diagnosis of a mental illness, and he or she is denied admission to a program or dismissed because of his or her diagnosis, the school is in violation of the law. Students should contact the compliance office or the ADA coordinator at their school or the OCR (see Chapter 3) to report such an incident.

If a student is having difficulty in a class and needs an accommodation (e.g., extended time for tests), an instructor cannot refuse to provide that accommodation if it is requested by or under the auspices of the DS office. However, instructors do have the right to deny a request from an individual student if it has not come through official channels, even though the student may have a right to that particular accommodation.

If a student becomes symptomatic on campus and causes an incident or if the student becomes disruptive and interferes with the functioning of the college or someone else's learning, he or she is subject to sanctions as identified in the student code of conduct. Students with psychiatric disabilities must be given the same due process as any other student on campus. However, if it is determined that the student is a hazard to the health and safety of others, he or she may be dismissed. The key in all situations is that due process must be followed. People cannot be made to leave campus simply because they have a mental illness. However, having a mental illness does not mean people are not responsible for their actions.

MAKING THE DECISION TO DISCLOSE

The decision to disclose a psychiatric disability may be a difficult one. Some educational institutions, even though it is against the law, are not very hospitable to students who have a history of mental illness. They may not be obviously discriminatory, but they also may not be very helpful. A school's openness to students with psychiatric disabilities can best be determined by talking to other students who have the same or similar diagnoses. Another clue is how well services to students with disabilities are advertised. A call to the DS office may be very helpful in determining not only the attitudes of the staff but also the kinds of services available.

Some students may be turned off by identifying themselves as "disabled." Each person must weigh the pros and cons of such an affiliation. DS has a mandate to provide services and accommodations to level the playing field for all students. This means that the services provided can help students with psychiatric disabilities compensate for whatever impairment they may have because of their illness. The services are usually provided by dedicated professionals who are trained in disability services and the law. There are many benefits to identifying oneself as a student with disabilities, and doing so will likely enhance the probability of meeting one's educational goal.

The Department of Mental Health of the state of Connecticut (1995) developed guidelines for disclosure. The following questions are adapted from those guidelines:

- Do the benefits of disclosure outweigh the risks of discrimination?
- Does the student have access to information about his or her rights against discrimination?
- Will the student's level of stress increase dramatically as a result of disclosure?
- Does the student anticipate support or hostility?
- Will the student be labeled? Will he or she know how to confront this labeling?
- Will the student be more comfortable once he or she is "out" as a person with a psychiatric history?

Students also must decide whether they will disclose their disability to their instructors or to other students. Many students who choose complete disclosure and adopt a willingness to talk about their illness have found acceptance from other students. For example, a student at one institution said, "There was this guy in my course that was very friendly with me and we got to know each other very well and I talked to him about my history, and he was very interested in it, and we are still friends to this day" (Dougherty et al., 1996, p. 64). Other students have written about their illnesses for papers or given reports that have disclosed information about themselves and found that both the instructors and students were very understanding. One student offered his perspective in the following terms:

> My advice is to keep it out in the open because I gave a presentation about Laurel House (a clubhouse program) and I got an "A" on the paper. I talked all about Laurel House and all about the whole program and I got an "A" and no one laughed and everyone was interested. Everybody was very interested in what I was talking about and they really liked me and they really thanked me for doing that. (Dougherty et al., 1996, pp. 62–63)

Many instructors and students are touched by the courage and determination it takes for students with psychiatric disabilities to return to school. However, it is important for students to consider how they will feel if they do not get the acceptance they want. It is important to use discretion before disclosing and to try to anticipate first how others will respond.

Many educational institutions, particularly community colleges, are very open and very helpful to students who have a history of mental illness. Most community colleges define their mission as being a resource to all people in their community. They welcome diversity and see it as a way of enriching the total education process for everyone.

FUNDING THE RETURN TO SCHOOL

A very real problem in returning to school is determining how to pay for tuition, books, transportation, and all of the related costs of an education. (See Chapter 8 for a detailed discussion on funding that is available for postsecondary education.) Some people who have decided to return to school have defaulted on previous school loans. Usually, their illness has made it impossible to both continue with school and work to pay off their loans. Although they are usually ineligible for further loans, in many cases if they have a verifiable disability, the previous loans can be forgiven. DS staff can usually be helpful in this process, or the institution that made the loan can be contacted for information regarding the forgiveness of the loan.

It also is advisable to begin school with a grant (e.g., a Pell grant) rather than a loan, until students are well established and successful in a school environment. Local VR departments can also assist with school expenses so loans do not have to be taken initially.

It is very important that students keep copies of all papers related to financial aid. This includes all correspondence with the Social Security Administration and VR. Documentation of all transactions is vital to avoid confusion, delays, and questions arising about sources and uses of funding. Complete and accurate copies can avoid headaches and heartaches further down the road.

STRATEGIES FOR A SUCCESSFUL RETURN

Returning to studying and concentrating after years away from school can be difficult. However, there is help available for people with psychiatric disabilities who may have problems learning certain kinds of material or mastering certain skills. Table 9.1 presents a list of problems students have identified and possible accommodations/services available in most schools to assist with overcoming them.

Some students may have trouble with particular classes such as foreign languages or math. A class can be waived if it is not deemed essential to the course of study; for example, a foreign language requirement may be waived for a student who is unable to retain large amounts of memorized material. Some classes are more easily waived than others. Math courses are more difficult to get waived because math is essential to many study programs. However, substitutions may be made in both cases, and alternative classes may be taken.

Medications are often cited as being a source of problems. Students may experience lethargy, be unable to get up for early morning

Table 9.1. Returning to school: Difficulties and accommodations/services

Difficulty	Accommodation/service
Registration	Peer/staff support
Financial aid	Peer/staff support
Lines and crowds	Priority registration
Selecting classes	Academic counseling
Taking notes	Study skills class Tape recorders Notetakers
Concentrating	Notetakers Books on tape
Taking tests	Testing accommodations
Comprehending	Learning disabilities testing and training
Parking	Special parking permit
Panic attacks in class	Seating changes, extra breaks
Managing internal distractions	Symptom management class

Source: Stringari (1996).

classes, experience dry mouth, lack endurance, or have trouble concentrating. Other students may have difficulty remembering or staying focused long enough to read a whole page of material.

Although these problems are serious, studies have indicated that medications are much more helpful than problematic (Wilson, 1996). The studies also have shown that medications increase rather than limit the ability of the brain to function. The side effects of medication may require a change in lifestyle, study, and learning styles, but accommodations and careful planning can help. Careful consideration should be given to medication changes during the semester. Changes can disrupt functioning and routines, resulting in poor performance and increased anxiety. Students should discuss the timing of all medication changes with their doctors to maximize their ability to learn and maintain a school routine.

Another problem students have identified is depression or mania related to the time of year, such as an anniversary of a loss or a particular season. Again, accommodations can be helpful; by modifying due dates for papers or tests or carrying a lighter class load during particularly stressful times, students can greatly enhance their chances for success.

Before returning to school, students may not have had to keep to a schedule. They may have been able to sleep late and complete chores at their own pace. Returning to school requires a formal schedule if a student is going to attend classes and complete assignments on time. An important but simple support is to help students develop an hourly schedule for each week of classes, including time for studying; time for recreation and relaxation; and time for sleeping, eating, and preparing good meals. A monthly or semester schedule is also helpful, including due dates for major assignments or tests and the time set aside to prepare for them. Planning ahead can reduce anxiety, provide a sense of control, and even improve grades.

Stable housing can also support being successful in school. Although some students have enrolled or continued in school when they have been homeless, in most cases it is easier to focus and study when housing is secure. A place set up for studying that is quiet, well lit, and has a table or desk and a comfortable chair will also make schoolwork easier and studying more productive.

MANAGING STRESS

Managing the stress associated with returning to school is crucial for people who have a history of mental illness. If stress is not kept within reasonable limits, it can trigger a hospitalization at a critical time during the semester. But even this step—returning to the hospital as needed—indicates self-understanding and acceptance and should be seen as part of a growth and recovery process.

Each person needs to be aware of his or her own stress triggers and be able to identify the warning signs that his or her stress levels are overloaded. Because stress may result in an increase in symptoms, effective stress management is essential to success. Some common warning signs of stress include the following: disturbed sleep, changes in appetite, changes in mood, changes in thoughts or feelings, and changes in behavior. Table 9.2 lists other clues that identify stress. Returning to school requires that students become responsible for their physical *and* mental health. Managing stress means looking at stress patterns and management strategies, developing a lifestyle that enhances health, and building a strong support system. It is important to know when to reach out for help. Asking for support earlier rather than later often keeps stress from building.

It is often recommended that prior to developing a plan to manage stress, students keep a log of the stressors in their lives, noting what caused stressful situations and how they felt when they happened. By becoming aware of the causes of stress and how they were affected by them, students can develop a plan to eliminate these triggers, and they can develop different responses to those they can't eliminate.

Positive self-talk—talking to oneself about one's feelings regarding a situation and then reframing the situation in a different light that is positive rather than negative—can be a valuable tool for students prone to stress. For example, if a student receives a low grade on a test, he or she may tell him- or herself that he or she is learning how to take tests, adapting to being in school again, and learning something from the ex-

Table 9.2.   Clues that identify the presence of stress

Physical stress	Emotional stress
Dizziness	Anxiety
Headaches	Drug and alcohol abuse
Grinding teeth, clenching jaws	Feelings of worthlessness
Tight muscles	Inability to concentrate
Rising blood pressure	Inability to slow down
Pounding heart	Nightmares
Perspiration	Nervousness
Upset stomach	Restlessness
Frequent urination	Depression
Clammy hands	Irritability
Fatigue	Confusion
Sleeplessness	Agitation

Source: Sequoia Hospital (cited in the County of San Mateo Mental Health Services, n.d.).

perience that will help with the next test. This is more helpful than telling him- or herself that he or she is stupid, should know better, or doesn't belong in school anyway. The first strategy will put the situation in a more positive, realistic light; the second strategy will cause stress.

There are many other things that students can do to manage stress, but they may involve making major lifestyle changes. Lifestyle changes are difficult but may be worth the effort to achieve an important goal. The National Institute of Mental Health recommended 10 strategies for relieving stress (Kopolow, 1991):

1. *Try physical activity.* When stressed, release the pressure through exercise. Walking, running, or doing some work at home will relieve the uptight feeling. The mind and body work together.
2. *Share your stress.* It helps to talk to someone about concerns and worries. Knowing when to ask for help may avoid more serious problems later.
3. *Know your limits.* If a problem is beyond your control and cannot be changed at the moment, do not fight the situation. Learn to accept what is—for now—until such time as you can change it.
4. *Take care of yourself.* Each person is special. Get enough rest and eat well. Poor physical health prevents people from dealing well with stress.
5. *Make time for fun.* Schedule time for both work and recreation. Play can be just as important to well-being as work.
6. *Be a participant.* People help themselves by helping others. Get involved in the world, and people will be attracted to you.

7. *Check off your tasks.* Trying to take care of everything at once can seem overwhelming. Make a list of the tasks to do, then do them, one at a time, checking them off as they are completed.

8. *Try cooperation.* Must you always be right? Do other people upset you, particularly when they will not do it your way? Try cooperation instead of confrontation.

9. *Let yourself cry.* A good cry can be a healthy way to bring relief to anxiety, and it might even prevent a headache or other physical consequence. It can be a healthy release in an otherwise uncontrollable situation.

10. *Create a quiet scene.* A quiet country scene painted mentally or beautiful music can create a sense of peace and tranquillity.

Deegan (1988), a consumer and professional, provided advice on promoting recovery during a speech at Merrimack College in North Andover, Massachusetts. In her speech, Deegan offered the following activities as helpful in promoting recovery:

- Intermittent or ongoing treatment
- Good working relationship with a psychologist, psychiatrist, and/or social worker
- Self-help groups for those who have used or abused drugs or alcohol
- Social or VR programs
- Friendships based on love and respect
- Participation in a spiritual community
- Participation in a consumer-run support network

Copeland, another consumer and professional who has worked with individuals with depression, said, "It became very clear to me . . . that those people who personally take responsibility for their own wellness achieve the highest level of stability, the highest level of awareness, control over their own lives, and happiness" (1992, p. 41).

Managing stress is a critical component for a student to be successful on campus. It may require changes in interpreting life experiences, being very methodical about tracking one's symptoms, and major changes in lifestyle. However, the changes will support all aspects of the person's life as well as enhance the educational process.

MAKING FRIENDS ON CAMPUS

Returning to school, under the best of circumstances, can be a scary and lonely endeavor. It is often a new and unfamiliar environment. New students may feel alone and isolated. If a student is attending only one class, opportunities to get to know other students may be limited. At the beginning, it is helpful for new students to take a career orientation class or a reentry class, not only for what will be learned but also because these classes provide opportunities to get to know other students. Classes in which there is a lot of interaction, such as an activities class or a discussion class, are the most helpful for students seeking new friends.

Some students meet other students at learning centers or through school activities such as special interest clubs or intramural sports teams. Some returning students may find that they are older than many other students and will want to attend adult or evening classes initially so they are with people who are more their peers in terms of age. Being accepted seems to be a function of getting to know people rather than a function of the mental illness.

One of the most valuable ways to learn new skills and make friends on campus is through a peer support group. Peer support groups are available on some campuses or through some mental health centers. If a peer support group is not available on a campus, one can be started with the help of an instructor of a reentry class, a DS staff member, or a mental health provider. A helpful resource manual for information on how to develop a peer support group is "Peer Support on a College Campus." (See the Appendix at the end of this book for further information on how to contact this group.)

COPING WITH FAILURE

Failure, similar to many other things, is in the eyes of the beholder. Changing class schedules to reduce work load and leaving school temporarily are sometimes necessary adjustments to manage a situation. The nature of a mental illness is often unpredictable, and the nature of the recovery process uneven; both need to be dealt with realistically.

One of the most common problems students face is difficulty in a class. Some education staff recommend students drop a class if failure seems probable. However, there are usually deadlines for how late classes can be dropped. Instructors will occasionally allow students with mental illness to do extra work so that they can pass a class.

Sometimes it may be necessary for students with psychiatric disabilities to reduce their course loads because of stress or other circumstances that may prevent them from giving the time necessary to do all the required work. Dropping a class does not demonstrate failure but rather a reassessment of what can be accomplished successfully at the time. It can be a means by which a student can learn more about him- or herself, or it can help him or her to assess what type of work load is manageable over time. Having to drop a class may also tell the student that stress is building and that some adjustments need to be made. Dropping a class is a healthy recognition of what the student needs.

The same is true for leaving school. Sometimes it is necessary to leave school—perhaps to rest, to be hospitalized, or to manage one's personal business; however, timing is important. In order to minimize the disruption, certain things need to be taken care of. Most colleges and universities have a medical leave policy. The college catalog may contain a copy of the policy or DS staff may have access to a copy. Sometimes special provisions can be made because of the episodic nature of a mental illness. Regardless of the policy, if a student is experiencing extreme difficulty in a class or in school in general and plans to leave school, he or she should do the following:

- Contact the financial aid office to minimize the disruption of financial aid and/or to make arrangements for loan repayments.
- If it is still early in the semester, request tuition and fee refunds.
- Contact instructors to arrange for incompletes rather than failures. Usually there is a 1-year grace period to complete the work. If the student does not plan to return, drop classes rather than let them become failing grades on transcripts.
- If residing in student housing, request refunds for fees and services paid for.

Realistically, a student may not be able to make all these arrangements him- or herself. Staff from the DS office, a mental health provider, a friend, or a family member can be helpful.

SUMMARY

Although it has been a long time in coming, more and more people with psychiatric disabilities are returning to college every day. Being a student with a psychiatric disability is no longer so unusual. All over the United States, schools are recognizing that there is a new group of individuals on campus. On some campuses, students with psychiatric disabilities are the second largest group of students with disabilities, exceeded only by those who have learning disabilities. Many years ago, it was unusual for women and racial minorities—not to mention people with physical disabilities—to attend college. Then, people with learning disabilities, an invisible disability, began to attend.

Each group had to make a place for itself in a sometimes unwelcoming environment. Now, one of the last groups of individuals to achieve its place on the campus is individuals with psychiatric disabilities. Although it has taken time, receiving an education is a civil right and cannot be taken away from individuals with psychiatric disabilities. What remains is full-scale acceptance as students and staff on campus recognize that once again, diversity will enrich and enhance their educational experience.

REFERENCES

Americans with Disabilities Act (ADA) of 1990, PL 101-336, 42 U.S.C. §§ 12101 *et seq.*

Copeland, M.E. (1992). *The depression workbook: A guide to living with depression and manic depression.* Oakland, CA: New Harbinger Publications, Inc.

County of San Mateo Mental Health Service. (n.d.). *Advanced Peer Counseling Manual.* San Mateo, CA: Author.

Deegan, P. (1988, July). *Recovery, rehabilitation and the conspiracy of hope: A keynote address.* Paper presented at The Partnership Moving Forward Conference, Merrimack College, North Andover, MA.

Department of Mental Health of the State of Connecticut. (1995). *Disclosure.* Hartford: Department of Mental Health, State of Connecticut, Office of Communications/Community Education.

Dougherty, S., Kampana, K., Kontos, R., Flores, M., Lockhart, R., & Shaw, D. (1996). Supported education: A qualitative study of the student experience. *Psychiatric Rehabilitation Journal, 19*(3), 59–70.

Kopolow, L. (1991). *Plain talk about handling stress.* Washington, DC: National Institute of Mental Health, Office of Scientific Information, Government Printing Office.

Rehabilitation Act of 1973, PL 93-112, 29 U.S.C. §§ 701 *et seq.*

Stringari, T. (1996). *Supported education: A definition.* Unpublished manuscript, College of San Mateo, CA.

Unger, K. (1997). *Inside the system.* Unpublished manuscript, Portland, OR.

Wilson, M. (1996, Winter). Dual diagnosis of psychological and learning disabilities: The role of psychotropic medication in assessment and treatment of learning disabilities. *Issues in Psychological Disabilities, A Collection of Readings prepared for the 1996 AHEAD TRIO Training Program* (pp. 8–9). Columbus: OH: Association on Higher Education and Disability.

10

Personal Experiences

From Onset to Recovery

We must recognize that persons with psychiatric disabilities do not "get rehabilitated" in the same sense that cars "get tuned up." Persons with psychiatric disabilities are not passive objects which professionals are responsible for "rehabilitating." It places responsibility in the wrong place. It perpetrates the myth that we are not and cannot be responsible for our own lives, decisions and choices. (Deegan, 1988)

Recovery does not refer to an end product or result. It does not mean that one is "cured." In fact, recovery is marked by an ever deepening acceptance of our limitations. But now, rather than being an occasion for despair, we find that our personal limitations are the ground from which spring our own unique possibilities. This is the paradox of recovery: i.e., that in accepting what we cannot do or be, we begin to discover who we can be and what we can do. Thus, recovery is a process. It is a way of life. (Deegan, 1988)

If you have come to help me you are wasting your time. But if you have come because your liberation is bound up with mine, then let us work together. (Watson, cited in Davidson, 1993, p. v)

It is difficult to imagine the experience of having a mental illness. Not only are people with mental illness treated by others as if they have literally lost their minds, but they also receive treatment from a system that can be both punitive and dehumanizing. Although many people receive excellent and caring intervention, others find that the intervention is as bad or worse than their illness. This is generally true not because individuals in the system are "bad" but because of outmoded ideas regarding both the cause and nature of mental illness and our understanding of the healing process. Unfortunately, human nature seems compelled to segregate certain people—by thought or by action—and to take away their humanity as well. In spite of some drawbacks within the mental health system, however, most people do benefit from the services it provides.

THE ONSET OF MENTAL ILLNESS

The onset of mental illness is extraordinarily frightening. Most people have no idea what is happening to them and are totally unprepared for the experience. Mosley (1994), a consumer and mental health professional, explained onset in these terms: "We don't plan to be ill. We don't study for it. Unless there is a convincing family history, we don't expect it, and we certainly don't desire it. And although we frequently joke about it, we never imagine that we might, someday, be insane."

The onset of a mental illness, which marks the beginning of a different kind of life for many people, often can manifest gradually over a period of many years. This period and the uncertainties and confusion that accompany the onset can be very stressful. One woman who may have had posttraumatic stress disorder as a child relates her life experiences in terms of her illnesses in the following terms:

> My life has been spent in and out of hospitals for many different mental traumas. . . . My recovery has been a long struggle, and I have many times almost died because of my actions. I would take something or do something to drown out my pains. My illness began when I was a child, but no one realized that I was sick. They did not know the effect my father abusing my mother had on me along with other family problems. At 12 years old, I began to have epilepsy and was not aware of it because of the lack of medical attention. My family doctor did not know or misdiagnosed me saying that I was having cramps and when I grew older and had children my suffering would stop. My recovery began in 1980 . . . when I was diagnosed with epilepsy, nervous breakdown, and, to top it off, I was listed as 55–50 "crazy." (Thomas, 1996, pp. 3–4)

For other people, the onset of a mental illness may manifest quickly over a period of weeks or months. This type of onset can be just as confusing as a more prolonged onset and can have just as devastating of an effect on a person. The following quote illustrates the power of an onset that occurred suddenly:

> One evening in the fall of 1971, as we were finishing our family dinner, the phone rang. I can remember getting up from my chair. That was the last thing I can remember until several weeks later, when I experienced flashing consciousness sufficient enough to understand that I was in the hospital. In fact, I had sustained an instantaneous manic episode! The next thing I can clearly remember, and this was weeks later, was a fleeting return to consciousness. I was in a quiet room in the cage of a mental ward. Although the entire period of hospitalization was to be remembered as one of occasional periods of foggy lucidity, I did come to understand that I had become mentally ill. I had lost my mind. I was forcibly detained, under the influence of "mental medications," and tentatively diagnosed as schizophrenic. (Berman, 1994, p. 40)

The onset of any major disease, such as diabetes, multiple sclerosis, or lupus, can be very frightening; most people typically have limited knowledge about these diseases unless they or a family member becomes ill. This, too, is usually the case with mental illness; no one is prepared for the experience. When individuals do not know what is happening, their lack of experience adds to the already terribly confusing and frightening experience. Crowley said, "I never experienced anything as terrifying as my mind failing me" (1996, p. 86). Another young woman described her feelings regarding mental illness in these terms:

> Limitless, spaceless, timeless, like the deep, the deep deep. Where no sun shines, no light exists, where creeping creatures slink to and fro, going nowhere, purposeless, lifeless, only because there is nothing left. Living off one another, devouring each other! Only they don't die, or dissolve, they are just digested and come back in other forms, haunting, taunting, terrorizing. (Penny, 1992, p. 26)

With the onset of a mental illness, people often lose the roles they once held as student, employee, and community member. They also may lose their senses of self-identity, their personalities, and their beliefs that they each have a unique personality. Instead, individuals feel a void and a sense of emptiness in their lives. They often feel as if no one understands them. A characteristic of some mental disorders is that people lose a sense of who they are, which leaves them feeling as if they are simply a disease without a real personality.

> My illness eradicated my sense of self, and now I am engaged in the lifelong process of obtaining, maintaining and slowly modifying my sense of who I am. (Anonymous, 1994, p. 25)

DIFFICULTIES WITH TREATMENT

When someone does develop a mental illness, the first step toward recovery is often hospitalization. Many hospitals have caring and knowledgeable staff with programs that are designed to help people return
home as soon as possible. Others are not as curative. Some individuals
in hospitals have had terrible experiences, which accounts for their belief that their treatment was worse than the original illness. The following are comments made by individuals who were hospitalized
after being diagnosed with a mental illness:

> As a young adult I was raped by a staff member of one of the institu-
> tions—so medicated no one thought I would know the difference. Anger
> wells up inside of me when I think that crime has to this day gone un-
> noticed. (Glater, 1992, p. 21)

> For two literally "hellish" years I was being worked over by the staff,
> many times being placed in four-point restraints (being tied stomach up-
> wards to a bed, with leather restraints at both wrists and ankles), being
> stripped of my clothing and being forced to spend hour upon hour in a
> "seclusion room" that stunk horribly of other people's urine, unable to use
> the men's room because some misguided patient liked to throw full rolls
> of toilet paper into the toilet. (Cloutier, 1994, p. 32)

A difficult aspect of being diagnosed with a mental illness is the
lowered expectations that other people have of you. Staff within the
mental health system may try to help consumers realistically assess
their futures, but the effect of a mental illness diagnosis can have long-
term negative effects. For example, one person was told the following:
"Your life is shattered. Permanently altered. Lower your expectations.
In reality being a good janitor has value" (Kim, 1992, p. 12).

People with psychiatric disabilities are unique, and their individual
abilities must be taken into account when developing their educational
and professional goals. If a person is placed in classes or at a worksite
that are below his or her capabilities, it can be quite devastating.

> They [the mental health system] don't really train people to do what they
> want to do, or find what their potential is. I went through a severe de-
> pression, was in a lot of pain. . . . Instead of sending me to school as a para-
> legal, they sent me to a sheltered workshop. I was standing next to some-
> one who was severely retarded and we were counting fish hooks. I was
> class president in college, I was a law school dropout. If I wasn't depressed
> going in, that sure did it. I thought, God, have I sunk this low? Is this what
> everybody thinks? (Reidy, 1994, p. 6)

Some mental health services providers may express their lack of
expectations and hopes for their consumers openly and thoughtlessly.

In doing so, they further discourage individuals who may be ready to move forward and rebuild their lives. The lowered expectations are often the result of the stigma surrounding a diagnosis of mental illness. Many people are not aware that although there may be impairments that result from the illness, most people can return to their typical lives; however, it is important to remember that each person's experience is different. It is this understanding of individual differences on which providers and counselors must draw in working with students to set realistic goals. A young woman with mental illness who earned a master's degree and is now a professional in the mental health field wrote the following about sharing her decision to go back to school with her mental health services provider:

> I clearly remember the day I told my mental health worker I was going back to school. He let out a short laugh, shook his head and said, "It's doubtful you will ever get a master's degree. If by some chance you do, you will never be able to use it. But I think you should take a class or two for socialization. Maybe a class in volleyball or a crafts class so you can be around other people. (Shepherd, 1993, p. 10)

THE RECOVERY PROCESS

People with psychiatric disabilities begin the recovery process for reasons that are as varied as the people themselves. Often it is another person who believes in them and treats them with kindness and respect. Sometimes the process is triggered by a particular experience or a series of lifestyle changes; other times it is new medications. Usually it is a combination of all of these factors. The initial experiences of recovery are often supported by the individual beginning a part-time job or volunteer work or returning to school. The realization that the process of recovery is beginning is often met with unexpected joy and a dramatic increase in hope and self-esteem. Often the best place to determine what began the process toward recovery or who helped the individual with the process is the individual him- or herself. One woman, who is a key person in the consumer movement, said the following:

> I take my medication and still have, what I call my "stop days" to regroup and recoup. Perhaps that's what recovery is all about—taking care of yourself. I accept my limitations and I don't like not being able to fully use my skill and capabilities. I live on SSI/SSA [Social Security Income/Social Security Administration] and I don't like that either. It's no fun not to have food at the end of the month. But I'm very rich too—in so many ways. On my good days (and I have many more of these) I function very well and I'm helping to make good things happen for myself and others. Actually, I feel this is when my recovery began . . . when I found a purpose in life. (Lee, 1994, p. 31)

Many clients have found that dedicated professionals in the mental health field were critical to the recovery process. It is often the professional's belief in the talents and abilities of the individual with a mental illness that inspire and sustain the individual's hope for rebuilding his or her life. Support often gives these individuals the courage and energy to try new ventures. The mental health system often provides a safe environment and a springboard from which to move forward. Zahn said, "The mental health system has been wonderful for me. It has been a shelter and help to get this far" (1996, p. 2). Professional encouragement and respect are invaluable during the recovery process of a person with mental illness. One woman described the importance of having her doctor listen to and respect her:

> Instead of questioning what prior doctors had called my "suspicious," "angry," and "paranoid" demeanor with regard to the medical profession, Lee's starting point was an assumption that my emotional state was rationally based. He treated me with respect. . . . By avoiding the natural tendency to downplay the insight and awareness of a mentally ill individual, he created an opportunity for mutual trust. . . . In a number of instances, Lee Jones accommodated my particular belief system and needs. . . . The cost of these accommodations was nominal. The value to my treatment was substantial. The empowering effect was incalculable. (Crowley, 1996, p. 87)

Many consumers have been helped by and learned from individuals with similar experiences. Informal peer support can be extremely effective in forming personal relationships and sharing experiences, knowledge, and friendships. For instance, knowing that other people have had problems or difficulty concentrating because of medications can help to make the experience less intimidating. Relationships can also be developed more formally among peer support groups in which people who have a mental illness come together to support and learn from one other. A former consumer described her first experience with a peer support group and her delight at finding the group so helpful in the following terms:

> I heard people in the peer group speak rationally about their school problems. The whole group LISTENED, and asked how they FELT about those problems, and LISTENED again. Then, as a group they talked over solutions and offered to help in ways that might be useful. No one told anyone else what to do. Serious problems that seemed to me psychiatric in origin and immovable were dispatched in 10 to 15 minutes. I was surprised to realize later that specific problems solved in this way never raised themselves again—they remained solved. People learned a new way of coping with a problem so they were comfortable with it. (Clark, 1993, pp. 198–199)

EDUCATION AND RECOVERY

In a peer support group, students can talk with an informal and understanding group of listeners about the difficulties of dealing with their disabilities in school. They can not only get useful advice but also share with others who have experienced the same things, which often lessens their burden.

> The hardest thing for me was my akathesia—the restless side effect of my medication. I would go to the student union, read for 15 minutes, then walk around for awhile, return to my seat, read for another 15 minutes and then repeat the cycle once more. (Orrin, 1997, p. 62)

Although sharing experiences and solutions to problems may help alleviate some of the feelings of frustration, formal assistance is also available at most universities in the form of accommodations (see Chapter 6). Accommodations can address problems related to concentrating on completing assignments on time, test anxiety, restlessness, early morning drowsiness, and other situations that make it difficult to succeed in a school environment. Students often do not realize how beneficial meaningful accommodations can be in helping to succeed in college or in graduate school.

> Having lectures taped makes a major difference. Sometimes I have to listen to each tape two or three times before I catch everything that's being said. Given this, I wonder how I ever understood what was happening in my previous classes. I realized my inability to comprehend the textbooks doesn't come from being disinterested or not smart enough to understand them, but from all the distractions happening in my head. . . . I requested flexibility regarding due dates. Flexible due dates have allowed me to turn in my assignments earlier or later so they are not all due at once. This helped me deal with the times of year when I have the most trouble—December and May—when it is hard for me to get anything done. (Shepherd, 1993, p. 10)

Recovery is achieved differently by each person, and each person begins from a different place. One dramatic success story is told by a former consumer who now works as a mental health professional. He also credited the help he received for allowing him to go back to school and get his master's degree.

> I have been a consumer of mental health services for 27 years with a diagnosis of Paranoid Schizophrenia. For three of those years I lived on the streets, floridly psychotic—sleeping in parks or on beaches. I begged for food and was jailed for vagrancy. I talked with aliens and spotted UFOs—spoke with Jesus and saw visions. I have been in remission for 11 years now and have been working as a counselor in mental health programs for six of those years.

My wife, who is also a consumer/student, and I recently bought our own house, and our son was just a year old this month. There was a time when living independently in a middle class lifestyle was not even something I could dream about, but supported education helped me set, and then go about achieving, goals that have altered the downward spiral that was my life. (Bruce, 1997, p. 52)

Regaining a productive life requires a renewed sense of oneself, a sense of self-sufficiency, and a clear vision of what one would like in his or her life. It means asking "What do I really want?" and then working toward that with persistence and hopefulness. Tenacity, determination, and using all of one's resources, including those available around him or her, are critical to this process.

I am one of the lucky ones. I have come back from years in the Twilight Zone of manic depression, and created a "Normal" life. In spite of almost 20 years of psychiatric care including a dozen medications, seven psychiatrists, four hospitalizations, a dozen lost jobs, and four interruptions in my schooling, I have graduated from college, established a career, renewed positive relations with my family, and been happily married for almost six years. I am not an extraordinary person. (Scheie-Lurie, 1992, p. 6)

People who have had a diagnosis of mental illness and are now recovering describe recovery as a process, one that may continue for the rest of their lives. With the process comes both an acceptance of whatever limitations there may be and a satisfaction of a life being well lived.

Through recovery I have found myself capable of making changes toward more satisfaction and success in my life. The quality of my life has greatly improved. I still have my limitations—I am not a finished product. And from an acceptance of my limitations has come a belief in my own unique possibilities. I have the power to move toward wholeness. (Walsh, 1996, p. 89)

My process of recovery had become the process of living life. . . . May the sharing of ourselves and our experiences, whether client, family member or professional, lead to greater respect for each of us and the individual paths we pursue. (Keil, 1992, p. 6)

Recovery is a personal experience that happens over time. With the continued development of new medications, more people will be going through the recovery process. Experiences have shown that personal support and opportunities also contribute to recovery. One of the most meaningful of those opportunities is returning to school.

Becoming a student provides people with mental illness the opportunity to take on one of the most valuable roles in American society—that of a student. Rather than being considered a "patient" or a "consumer," individuals can be viewed as a student at a college, university, or training program. Enrollment alone can be interpreted as the individual doing something productive and beneficial to his or her life. This change in identity can have a remarkable effect on people with mental illness. It can energize individuals and help them improve their sense of self-sufficiency and self-esteem. It can renew their determination, both to develop goals and strive to achieve them.

> Who would have thought that I would be so incredibly excited about my life? I'm going to the University and nothing and no one is going to stop me! I can learn! This is such an exciting and novel concept for me. I am able to understand ideas and concepts. (Gilbert, Heximer, & Walker, 1997, p. 25)

SUMMARY

People with a history of mental illness deserve respect and admiration. Although there are no "cures" for mental illness and no easy solutions to the residual effects of the disabilities, many people are able to resume many of their former roles and lead a fulfilling and successful life. Although the journey from onset to recovery is mostly personal, through the sharing of their experiences, people who have a mental illness have told us how we can be most helpful. We need to listen.

> A full range of quality, affordable services would significantly help most people with serious mental illnesses. Such services include medical care (both psychiatric and general), transitional programs like group homes, low cost housing, vocational support, social activities, self-help support groups, peers and appropriate educational experiences. Beyond these basic services, however, is the critical issue of quality of care. Sheer quantity of services will never make up for lack of quality. Without a correct philosophy of care, including a respectful attitude toward consumers and an understanding of the process of recovery, not even the most complete system will succeed. (Scheie-Lurie, 1992, p. 36)

Supported education is an important part of the full range of services that should be available to people with psychiatric disabilities. Supported education is not a difficult or extremely expensive service to provide. For the most part, the people and financial resources are already in place. The only thing that is required is a shift in attitude to utilize them.

Although the experience of mental illness can be debilitating, the people behind the voices expressed in this chapter have rebuilt their lives. Most are successful professionals who have learned the value of relationships. They have used their experiences to bring humanity and compassion to their work. Many are employed in the mental health profession, including psychiatrists, clinical psychologists, and directors of agencies. Others are employed as artists, paralegals, and computer specialists. Others are living independently and are in various stages of recovery. They are all living proof that positive attitudes, opportunities, and hope are important. They are a tribute to the human spirit.

REFERENCES

Anonymous. (1994). Coping and recovery. In L. Spaniol & M. Koehler (Ed.), *The experience of recovery* (pp. 24–25). Boston: Boston University, Center for Psychiatric Rehabilitation.

Berman, R. (1994). Lithium's other face. In L Spaniol & M. Koehler (Eds.), *The experience of recovery* (pp. 40–45). Boston: Boston University, Center for Psychiatric Rehabilitation.

Bruce, P. (1997). My experience with supported education. *The Journal of the California Alliance for the Mentally Ill, 8*(2), 52.

Clark, P. (1993). What's a nice editor like you doing in a place like this? *Psychosocial Rehabilitation Journal, 17*(1), 197–199.

Cloutier, G. (1994). Overcoming the black garden. In L. Spaniol & M. Koehler (Eds.), *The experience of recovery* (pp. 29–34). Boston: Boston University, Center for Psychiatric Rehabilitation.

Crowley, K. (1996). What is possible in psychiatry: Five psychiatric steps that mattered. *Psychiatric Rehabilitation Journal, 19*(4) 85–87.

Davidson, H. (1993). *Just ask: A handbook for instructors of students with mental disorders.* Calgary, Alberta, Canada: Detselig Enterprises, Ltd.

Deegan, P. (1988, July). *Recovery, rehabilitation and the conspiracy of hope: A keynote address.* Speech given at The Partnership Moving Forward Conference, Merrimack College, North Andover, MA.

Gilbert, R., Heximer, S., & Walker, M. (1997). Removing barriers to education. *The Journal of the California Alliance for the Mentally Ill, 8*(2), 28.

Glater, S. (1992). The journey home. *The Journal of the California Alliance of the Mentally Ill, 3*(2), 21–22.

Grimmer, K. (1992). The invisible illness. *The Journal of the California Alliance of the Mentally Ill, 3*(2), 27-28.

Keil, J. (1992). The mountain of my mental illness. *The Journal of the California Alliance of the Mentally Ill, 3*(2), 5–6.

Kim, D. (1992). They took my friend away. *The Journal of the California Alliance of the Mentally Ill, 3*(2), 12–13.

Lee, C. (1994). A flight from despair: An emergence. *The Journal of the California Alliance of the Mentally Ill, 5*(3), 30–31.

Mosley, L.E. (1994, September). *Education and persons with a psychiatric disability.* Speech presented at the Therapeutic Education Conference, San Diego, CA.

Orrin, D. (1997). How I earned my MSW despite my mental illness. *The Journal of the California Alliance of the Mentally Ill, 8*(2), 61–63.

Penny, C. (1992). Excerpts from my journal of madness. *The Journal of the California Alliance of the Mentally Ill, 3*(2), 26.

Reidy, D. (1994). Recovering from treatment: The mental health system as agent of stigma. *Resources, 6*(3), 2.

Scheie-Lurie, M. (1992). Recovery: It takes more than finding the right pill. *The Journal of the California Alliance of the Mentally Ill, 3*(2), 36.

Shepherd, L. (1993). School daze. *Psychosocial Rehabilitation Journal, 17*(1), 7–10.

Stanley, R. (1992). Welcome to reality: Not a facsimile. *The Journal of the California Alliance of the Mentally Ill, 3*(2), 25–26.

Thomas, M. (1996). *In and out of prison: From mental illness to recovery.* Unpublished class assignment, College of San Mateo, San Mateo, CA.

Walsh, D. (1996). Journey towards recovery. *Psychiatric Rehabilitation Journal, 20*(2), 85–89.

Zahn, A. (1996). Unpublished class assignment, College of San Mateo, San Mateo, CA.

Appendix

Human Services Resources

Association on Higher Education
and Disability (AHEAD)
Post Office Box 21192
Columbus, OH 43221
(614) 488-4972
Fax: (614) 488-1174

Financial Aid for Students with
Disabilities
HEATH Resource Center
One Dupont Circle, N.W.,
Suite 800
Washington, D.C. 20036
(800) 544-3284

Funding Your Education
Federal Student Aid Programs
Post Office Box 84
Washington, D.C. 20044
(800) 433-3243

International Association of
Psychosocial Rehabilitation
Services (IAPRS)
5550 Sterret Place, Suite 214
Columbia, MD 21044
(301) 730-7190

National Alliance for the
Mentally Ill (NAMI)
2101 Wilson Boulevard, Suite 302
Arlington, VA 22201
(703) 524-7600

National Mental Health
Association
1021 Prince Street
Alexandria, VA 22314
(703) 684-7722

Peer Support on a College
Campus
National Research and
Training Center
104 South Michigan Avenue,
Suite 900
Chicago, IL 60603

Social Security Administration
2100 M Street, N.W.
Washington, D.C. 20044
(800) 772-1213

The Student Guide—Financial
Aid from the U.S. Department
of Education
Federal Student Aid Programs
Post Office Box 84
Washington, D.C. 20044
(800) 433-3243

Index

Academic counseling, 92
Accessibility, 81–82
  barriers and, 82–84
  legislation relating to, 65–66
  as program value, 17–18
Accommodations, 67–76, 79–98
  acceptance into programs and
    services and, 158–159
  assistive devices, 69
  barriers to success and, 82–84
  defined, 63, 86–87
  disclosure and, 89–90, 159
  disruptive students and, 73–75
  goal setting and, 90–91
  home-based instruction, 69
  job, 131
  medications and, 89
  program models for, 95–98
  psychiatric withdrawal and,
    75–76
  recovery and, 175
  requests for, 63–64
    time allowed for response to,
      71–72
  special needs and, 84–90
  special programs, 73
  substitutions and waivers, 72–73
  successful return to school and,
    161–163
  testing-related, 69–71
  tutors, 68
ADA, *see* Americans with Disabilities
  Act of 1990 (PL 101-336)
Admission
  eligibility for, 81–82, 158
  readmission after leave of absence,
    67
    strategies for successful return,
      161–163
Affect
  flattened, in schizophrenia, 31

  handling of, borderline personality
    disorder and, 110
Age, at onset of mental illness, 24
  major depressive disorder, 33
  panic attacks, 35
  schizophrenia, 31–32
Agencies
  community coalitions of, 131–133
  funding for, 151–153
  Vocational Rehabilitation, financial
    aid from, 147–149
Aggression
  perceived dangers of, 42–43
    assessment and coping
      strategies for, 111–113
  verbal, 107
Agoraphobia, 35–36
  panic attacks and, 34, 36
Akathisia, medication causing, 48
Alcohol abuse, *see* Substance abuse,
  mental disorders and
Alcoholics Anonymous, 39
Alprazolam (Xanax), 52, 85
Americans with Disabilities Act of
  1990 (PL 101-336), 60–63
  admission and, 65–66, 81, 158
  compliance with, 62–63
  confidentiality and, 65
  documentation requirements and,
    64
  readmission and, 67
  substitutions and waivers and, 72
  testing and, 69, 70, 71
AmeriCorps program, 150
Antianxiety drugs, 51–52
  effects of, on learning, 85
Antidepressant drugs, 50–51
Antipsychotic medications, 49–50
  side effects of, 49, 50
    learning and, 86
  see also Medication